RATTLED AWAKE:

VOLUME TWO

Anthology

CONTENTS

INTRODUCTION

No matter what has happened over the past five years, allow optimism enter.

Each "Rattled Awake" moment can bring you a gift.

Enjoy the treasures each author shares so freely here, and let them inspire you to rewrite your next chapter.

RATTLED AWAKE:
VOLUME TWO

THAT AIN'T NO GENIE IN A BOTTLE! … LESLEY MOUTON

If I had stayed where I was, I'd either be dead or wearing orange, and that ain't my color, honey! This isn't my story, it's something that happened to me. You know, you wouldn't want to be defined by one incident, right? So, I'll share how my future saved me.

Do you ever look back on your life and wonder how you got to where you are? Is there a higher power that guides your footsteps or are we just wandering around aimlessly and hoping we make
it to the next destination in one piece…whatever that may look like?

When I was younger, I never had a plan or next step. I was enjoying life, the party life, to be exact. As a young girl of eighteen, in Louisiana, we could legally go to bars and drink. Boy oh boy did I ever! It was the way of it, so I thought. You went to school, worked all week and looked forward to partying it up with friends on the weekends. The weekends turned into going out on Thursdays, then Wednesdays, and ladies' nights were on Tuesdays, so let's take advantage of the free drinks. Mondays were 'catch-up on everything else' days.

This way of drinking, and not thinking, started taking its toll. You see, I was in my last year of high school. After being out drinking, it was getting harder and harder to go to class, usually because I was hung over the toilet bowl in the morning. Eventually, I quit going to school. You know what happens when you don't go? For some reason, they wouldn't just give me my diploma. Go figure! The night I watched my friends and schoolmates graduate without me should have been a wake-up call. Instead, I was chomping at the bit for it to be over so we could go out and celebrate! "Celebrate good times, come on!!"

After a couple of years of bouncing around from one job to another, and one bad relationship to another, my drinking and reckless behavior were out of control. When I tried to end the current relationship I was in, it proved certain that I needed to leave town. Two days later, my dad sent a plane ticket to meet he and my mom in California, where he was working.

California was a new way of life, a fresh start, a place to be a new me. Not long after being there, I befriended a cowboy my parents knew, and we started dating. Our backgrounds were totally different, but we fell in love and had a great time together. We traveled to Louisiana, Arizona, and New Mexico to meet his family. After his job opportunity didn't work out there, he had no choice but to send me back to California. Because I was hurt and wanted to be with him, not back with my parents, my drinking was what I turned to. It was familiar and helped me forget the pain I was feeling. He came back to get me, and I was so stubborn, I refused and totally messed things up!

Insert more drinking, more bad choices, and lots of dance music here.

Some months went by, and I eventually moved back to Louisiana. The drinking continued while I hopped from one job to another, again. At one point, I had coworkers covering for me on Saturdays while I was in the bathroom at work hungover! Not a pretty sight, but it never slowed me down. Usually, after a good meal and a shower, I was back out in the bars again.

A year or two went by and most of it was a blur. I moved back and forth with my parents to Florida and Alabama and back to Louisiana. The partying, drinking and never knowing my next step continued. "Life is a highway, I'm going to ride it, all night long!"

My friends were all getting married and having kids; this is something I should be doing, right? I started dating Shawn, a guy that I dated briefly in high school. It was a good time, all the time, and involved lots of partying. Something familiar to me and we rolled with it! Within a year's time, we were married and expecting a baby. A baby? Whoa!!!! Sober alert! Sober alert!

Nailed it! We're parents! I'm a mom! I fell in love with being a mom in every way possible. My daughter was such a Godsend and blessing to me. I stayed sober longer than I had since I was eighteen. There I was, 26 years old and seeing life differently.Six years later we created another beautiful daughter. Life was good!

During those years, I did drink. Granted, my drinking never took over, but there was plenty of drinking.

Being the wife of a man who worked offshore, a man who was there more than home, had its stresses. Life has stressors. Family, bills, outside influences, marriage, and just life can be stressful for an individual and marriage alike. We all have them. I had two girls to raise and here I was a full time/part-time wife and mom.

Stress, from time to time, would be my excuse to drink. Honestly, I don't even think I used it as an excuse. I just did it. Like, there's no shame in my game, sista! You coming over to visit and we're drinking, friend. The more the merrier! No real conversation or anything going on. I was a caretaker to those around me. End of story! "It's a party over here, a party over there, shaking our derriere!"

Growing up and living in Louisiana is different. Our culture and way of living, especially in South Louisiana, revolves around eating and drinking. Life is a party and us Cajuns do it up big big! Laissez les bons temps rouler! (let the good times roll)

Fast forward 25 years. My husband was already home a lot after the oilfield started slowing down. The new Obama administration stopped all deep-water offshore drilling and made things harder and harder for these offshore companies to keep their heads above water. A few years later entered COVID...the big C, and I don't mean cancer. That really put a halt on most companies and most people everywhere. Due to the pain this still causes me, I won't give the big C any more power than that by discussing it further.

Looking back now, I feel God put some specific things in place for Shawn and me. Even though we were feeling the effects of what was going on in the world, we spent more time together in those six months than ever before in our whole marriage. We went out for dinner and drinks together. We played cards and dice together while cooking and listening to music. We got to take a trip to the beach in celebration of our 25th wedding anniversary. We laughed more. We shared good times together. Little did we realize the big-C curveball headed our way a few months later - one that would bring our happiness to an end. "Turn the Page."

Being the awesome provider Shawn was, he took a side gig, along with his brother, doing some outside work. It was hot and he'd come home exhausted. After the fourth day, he came in and went straight to bed. I knew he was sick! A few days later he was in the hospital, fighting for his life, alone! Eleven days later, pneumonia stopped his heart. Shawn was gone.

How do you go on? How do you go from we to me? How is this real? I couldn't fathom it, yet I was living it. I was questioning it daily. I tried to wrap my head around it but couldn't. I would no longer feel his arms around me to tell me everything was going to be ok. Just trying to breathe hurt!

The days before, during, and after his funeral were the hardest thing my girls, his son, and I have been through ever in our lives. This isn't supposed to happen! How do we get through it? Did this just happen? I made us all promise we'd get through it together.

My preacher told me to pray. Pray? I can't even speak to God right now! He didn't answer our prayers and heal Shawn!

The funeral home gave me a pamphlet on the five stages of grief. So, when I get through those five stages I'll be over my grief? Um…NO!

People suggested group grief counseling. No way could I go and hear everyone's story, let alone having to share mine all the time. YUCK!

Of course, I was told by do-gooders that I should smile, be happy because he'd want me to be. More advice rolled-in: find a hobby, take a trip, sell his things, hold on to his things, talk about him, don't talk about it, stay home, go out, be strong for my kids, let your kids see your pain, let him go so his soul can be released, never forget him, and so on and so on.

How about this? Do NOT give advice to someone who can't even think straight. Just let them be in their grief. Just be by their side. Do NOT try to compare your loss to someone else's (it's not a competition.) Talk about him. Don't try to act like it didn't happen. Cry with them. No need to say anything, except maybe "Les, I know you're in pain, but I'm concerned about your drinking. I love you and don't want to see anything bad happen to you!" Crickets! I know it wasn't anyone else's responsibility to get me to quit drinking. They were dealing with their own junk, too.

Good ole alcohol didn't let me down, though! It was always there for me. 'Numbed my pain, so I thought. 'Made me feel normal, or so I thought. I could act somewhat happy when drinking. Fake! Okay, now I'm getting somewhere. Keep drinking and others will think you're okay and quit with all the advice and poor pitiful looks they were giving me. This may work!

Good grief, girl! When you get home, you're still without him. That's not changing. When you wake up, you're still without him! You're still without him when you're driving home drunk every night! And being drunk at the bar at the end of the night crying to the bartender is not a pretty sight, momma!

I didn't give myself any other choice. Drinking, and going to the bar, was my new thing. That's what I was doing to replace the pain. That's what I was doing to try to feel normal. If someone wanted to see me, they came to the bar. We'll drink! "Shots, Shots, Shots, Shots, Shots, Shots… everybody!" A year and a half later, I was still doing shots.

Do you ever get the feeling that certain things happen for a reason? I never gave it much thought, until recently. I awoke from a dream that seemed extremely real to me. To this day, I can't even remember what it was about, only who it was about: Vincent, my cowboy from California. I couldn't get him out of my mind. Since I no longer had his sister's number, I searched for her on Facebook. I reached out to his other sister there and asked her to give him my number. A few hours later I received a text message. "Hey, stranger!"

Lots of text, lots of calls, lots of laughs, lots of tears! I was feeling alive again. Happy again. Loved again! "Cowboy Take me Away!"

One night while on the phone, he mentioned being upset that I was drunk and had driven myself home. He pointed out the obvious: that I was still getting drunk after all these years. HMPH! That did NOT sit well with me. Obviously, the truth hurts! You ever hear something, ignore it, yet it plays over and over again in your mind? That's where I was at!

A couple of months later, I made the decision to quit drinking. WHAT? Gosh, I was SO sick some days. I would cry, shake, feel like I had the flu, and ate lots of sweets. All the while, Vince would talk me through it. He'd encourage me, and make fun so I'd laugh, too.

The real work was being sober in front of my friends. No one could understand how, and they questioned why. They blamed Vince for forcing me to stop drinking and start back on a keto diet. Still today, I can't wrap my head around why they couldn't be happy for me. Why couldn't they encourage me? Why couldn't they support me to be a better version of myself?

The saying goes that friends will come and go along with the seasons of our lives. I believe that. People as a whole change, along with their current life situations and location. We weren't created to stay in one place. Childhood friends move on. High School friends move away to different colleges or towns to start their adult lives. Some start families and have kids. Can we relate to all those at once? Of course not! Everyone either grows or remains the same. Sometimes we shed friends just as a tree sheds their leaves and grows new ones. And if we're fortunate enough, we'll have a few from beginning to end. Friends that remained and supported the sober, healthier me, will always have a special place in my heart and my life.

There are times in our lives when we struggle with things. Mine, apparently, has always been alcohol. Never seeing it as a problem is a problem. Drinking on a normal basis is a problem. Using it to numb the pain is a problem. I had a problem. Never ever not one day was I concerned that my girls were watching me. That was a problem. I see that now!

Going from drunk to sober, from grief to happiness, from living in my hometown to moving away from my girls has not been easy. Perfection isn't my jam, and I should never fool myself to think I could or should be perfect. There is no such thing. I am human.

The grief of losing Shawn has never gone away, nor do I expect it to. One cannot just wake up and be done with grief. When your heart loves deeply, it grieves deeper!

The happiness of reconnecting with Vince comes with its own challenges, especially when my mind goes back to what took place for me to be where I am now: happy and loved! Allowing your heart to feel joy and happiness after losing someone is an ongoing struggle. You can feel like you don't deserve love and happiness. You can have feelings of guilt. It can feel like cheating at times, also.

Happiness can look like so many different things to so many people. I do know it will never be at the bottom of a bottle. For me, finding happiness within myself is what's important and it's a work in progress. I mean, after all, aren't we that on a daily?

During grief, we should continue to eat healthily, sleep when we can, get outside and do some light exercise, meditate, pray, and let grief happen! Dealing with grief can look like so many different things to so many different people. There's no right way to do it. I do believe there is a healthy way to do it. There's a non-destructive way to handle it, also. Looking back, I wish I had chosen the healthier option and not be looking for the genie at the bottom of a bottle.

When asked to share my rattled awake moment, the first thing I thought of was how my life was flipped upside down the day my husband passed away. In reality, my rattled awake moment was when my long history of drinking was shoved in my face, and I was left with those thoughts. It's something I sit with daily. Dealing with it is what I'm doing. Triumphant on most days. Working toward it daily!

Alcohol, drugs or other substances people abuse can be like a thief in the night. They can rob you of your joy, your memory, money, family and your friends. Abuse of alcohol or drugs can ruin relationships, jobs, and your health. Looking back at how I looked in the past to now, alcohol has left a timeline on my face and body that can't be erased. I can, however, erase the damage inside it may have caused with the right supplements, nutrition, exercise, right choices and most importantly, love for myself.

I hope and pray if you are reading this and have a struggle that keeps you reaching for that drink that you'll reevaluate it. Don't ever think you're alone. Don't ever think it's too hard. Don't ever think you're not good enough to be sober. Reach out to someone. Anyone, except for the drunk at the local bar...they'll just order you a drink!

Lesley Mouton is on a mission to help others create a healthier version of themselves, holistically. For over five years she has enhanced the lives of others through education and wellness by helping them reach their goals. Lesley is a best-selling coauthor in the book "Wise Women: Mother, Maiden, Crone." She is a mother of two grown girls and one granddaughter. Lesley's blog, VastLegacies.com details story worthy travel moments made as she, two dogs and her boyfriend traverse the US interviewing people who still do traditional cowboy arts. You can find her at or on LinkedIn www.linkedin.com/in/lotusholisticsolutions

THIS HAS TO STOP... BOB WITTY

A True Story About Veteran Suicide

I called on my way over, no answer. He lived a few doors down and as I walked up his garage was open, so I walked in. I went into the living room and I could see his legs behind the couch and the blood splatter on the wall. Took a second to realize what happened but I didn't want to take another step further. I called 911 immediately and a friend that I called on the way over, then I waited for the cops. Some young rookie asked me why didn't I check to see if he was alive and I snapped at him, "Are you kidding? Did you see what's on the wall?!" and I walked away. It wasnt the first suicide I've experienced, but it was a very violent one. It was so intense it became a calling and one of the things that persuaded me to get involved with the veteran suicide program.

Reflecting on my time here paints a picture of solitude, friends and family are not very close. I met Joe at the VA about 3 years ago and he was assigned to the same temporary VA housing complex. He was a few years older but it seemed we were meant to be friends. We hung out, went to groups together, watched sports and ate a lot of pizza. He was a cool guy, and we connected.

As I got to know him better, there was a period of time I sensed something was wrong. I recognized changes in his mood, erratic behavior, he was bailing on groups. This immediately heightened my senses because I had been there before. We had spoken about going down to the shooting range a couple times. I had to ask him about his guns and I knew the way he looked at me that he knew why I was asking and he said "Hey, man, don't worry everything's cool, just been a little bit tired." I asked him to go to a group with me, but they called the group off because it happened to coincide with the first day the VA shut down for Covid. I called him early in the morning and the plan was to go over to his house and sit on Zoom together and do the zoom group.

Gave him a quick call before I went over and he didn't answer. I called him again and he didn't answer. I went over to his house and my wheels were turning - I just felt like something was wrong. I called another friend over at the VA and I said "You know what man? Stand by the phone because I have a bad feeling about this." I hated to be right.

PTSD hits people in many different ways. For me, it was an array of disorders individually but seemingly all coming at the same time. I had anxiety, depression and panic attacks. even hypervigilance and OCD. My understanding was that PTSD was just one thing but I was wrong: PTSD rained disorders on me and I was thrown for a loop, confused because I didn't know one disorder from the other.

Joe and I often talked about this and he had his own challenges. He was a Vietnam vet, just a few years older than me, so he caught the tail end of the war in 1975. He told me it was pretty brutal and he had flashbacks. One time I saw him and how he reacted and I saw the look on his face. It's like he stepped into another dimension and actually was in the war at the time but it was in his home. He acted like he was taking fire from the enemy, and was hiding from them. I started to think, *was there no end to this?*

Well one thing I do know is that if everything ends, there is also a beginning. And I can tell you that beginning for us veterans is group therapy... and one thing for sure is that group therapy is a blessing for all of us. I've been attending many veterans' groups and the camaraderie that we have, because of what we have been through, is a special bond. I've seen people turn the corner in groups. It's a therapy we offer each other just by being there and supporting each other. I've made relationships that will last the rest of my life. One thing we talked about quite often, because of the visibility, is veteran suicide, and could it be prevented?

I volunteered my way around the VA and one department that was very interesting was the Office of Mental Health and Suicide Prevention (OMHSP.) This department is the one that publicizes the suicide rate as we see it on a daily basis. All the data comes from the CDC from each state and it's very accurate. As you've probably heard, over the last few years the number is 23 per day on the average. I found out that the CDC database was publicly available and you could pay for access. I figured I'd take a look at the information myself. I started to dig deeper into reference materials from the database, where I found an NIH article; an abstract that stated success against the known suicide rate of 74% with firearms in the first year. I'm thinking to myself, *why don't more people know about this and how can I use these numbers?* This is a research database and there's tons of reference material and links and that's what was going on.

Then I found magic: the article of a country that had this very same problem as we do and successfully reduced their suicide rate by 50% in two years. It's an article from

Israel that talks about the IMF, which is their army. When they come home, they are screened just like our guys are screened; it is both a physical and a mental assessment. On the mental assessment, the returning soldier is given a score based on that score a time frame is allocated. That time frame is a safe period during that safe period the soldier is asked to turn in his firearm. Israel was facing a suicide rate of 60% in the first year and 75% of those soldiers committed suicide with a firearm. After 2 years the suicide rate went down 50% and saved thousands of lives. This just fueled my mission because there is a solution proven by another country that has similar stats and will save lives.

Here's my story:
I grew up and went to school in Northern California. The colleges were San Jose State and San Francisco State. For ten years, I served my country in the United States Air Force. I got married and raised three boys in Northern California. I surfed, skateboarded, windsurfed, wake boarded, wake surfed, rode dirt bikes, mountain bikes and fished relentlessly. We only fished offshore because we wanted to catch the biggest, most powerful fish. We were all about extreme sports and obviously mostly board sports. My kids were naturals, both great surfers, a great musician and a two-time National Snowboard Champion turned professional snowboarder who was fully sponsored and traveling around the world at 17 years old. The apple doesn't fall too far from the tree. I retired at 50 and had a great career during the tech boom in Silicon Valley. Within a couple of years, the plan was set.

I moved down to Costa Rica and opened up my first surf camp; several more as time went on. It was paradise. I had arrived and was living the dream. Surfing every day, doing yoga, running on the beach, eating fresh food and fresh fish. It was a wonderful lifestyle for 10 years. During that time, I traveled back and forth between Costa Rica and the United States to see my family, with my family coming down, as well. I surfed during the season, and came home to Lake Tahoe to snowboard.

During this incredible existence, while visiting the states, I fell down some stairs. It was the day that ended life as I knew it. The fall partially severed my spinal cord between C1 and C2, and severely damaged my back, head and neck; everything was interconnected.

Everything I loved to do was gone: no more surfing, no more of those pure adrenaline extreme sports. Now stuck in a chair most of the day, it was tough. For a little bit I read a lot of inspiring books by athletes that had taken a similar path and were able to overcome such adversity, but I could not. I tried, but maybe I didn't try hard enough. I had to learn how to live again: how to wash my face, brush my teeth, feed myself, dress myself and everything else that comes with that kind of injury. Loss of mobility, neuropathy issues, circulation issues, muscle spasms, loss of coordination, and tremors. I drop stuff all the time, have no dexterity, battle with cognitive and memory problems, and incontinence. That's my favorite and always fun.

I slowly got more miserable. I decided to walk away from the light and walk into the darkness of despair. It didn't serve me well. I was already taking painkillers and started drinking alcohol. It all turned into a train wreck pretty quickly. I got worse and worse until I was just hopeless, full of guilt, shame and despair. It was torture; I couldn't take it anymore, feeling that it was time to go; I didn't want any part of this life. I just wanted to end it and see that suicidal ideation through. I went through several months of that on and off. Finally, I did try to take my life with pills and alcohol. I took a very large amount of Oxycontin which would kill most people, drank alcohol and went to sleep praying I wasn't going to wake up. The next day, I started coming to, waking up to find the left side of my face stuck to the hardwood floor. I could barely could open my right eye, and when I, did I'm thinking, *F*** I'm still alive.*

Later that day I thought *'How could I possibly take my own life?* How could I possibly think like that? How can I do that to my family? How can I leave them like that? How can I leave that legacy with them?' I was tortured either way but I always had God on my side.

A Veteran's Experience: A lab rat caught in a maze
Bad combination - drugs and alcohol just don't sit well, but hey, I was like everybody else going through the revolving pill factory at the VA. Every day, I took 15 different pills and I never felt any different; never knew if they were working or not. The psychiatrists always say give it about 6 weeks or so and we will know then, but about 6-8 weeks would go by I didn't feel a thing. Well, if you didn't, let's try something else, they would say. Give it about 6 weeks and let me know. It happens again and again and they will continue to switch until you feel something. The reality is most doctors know that a majority do not work, and there is not much backing the efficacy of the rest.

In PTSD's favor what we have actually done a great job at is understanding trauma. Trauma comes in all forms and has no prejudice or friends. We all have some form of trauma and if you were fortunate enough not to experience it during your life, don't go celebrating yet because there is a very high probability that you have some form of generational trauma.

I thought about the Vietnam vets that are on the street, all those guys who have just been discarded, thrown in the trash and disrespected. There is a staggering prevalence of suicide among our veterans and why? Because the system which is entrusted for caring has failed us miserably.

I thought back to numbers. There is no denying the success that the IMF had, yet here we sit, with so many people and companies working so hard to bring down the average daily suicide rate without results. I have watched for three years, but for some reason the needle is still hovering around 23.

Now the motivation is piling up around me and that's *it* - I'm moving forward; I'm going to break the ice. It is time to do something. The numbers are there, the IMF proved it. While it is true the scenarios between the IMF and the US are slightly different, we can do something similar. I believe we can still achieve great success.

There are multiple factors being taken into consideration in the development of a US program for soldiers returning to civilian life:

- ✓ The Protocol Doc or Buddy System
- ✓ The Buddy System "Never Go Alone"
- ✓ Directory of other Vets or Buddies
- ✓ Vet Support Group
- ✓ Sponsorship

- ✓ Warning signs

- ✓ Stigmas

- ✓ Risk Factors

- ✓ Civilian Life with & without support

- ✓ Conversation Starters

- ✓ Safe Period

Here is why this matters so much

Given 23 as the number of veteran suicides today, yearly, that adds up to about 8,395 per year. What a *terrible number*. With implementation of a program similar to the IMF, we can anticipate saving nearly 2,500 lives a year. Even if it was 2,000, that is a huge win for our country. I know we can make it happen. The evidence is there and we just have to execute this simple program together. Keyword "together."

General Douglas MacArthur once said "In war, there is no substitute for victory." As a soldier this speaks to the resolve, determination and unwavering commitment to the Call of Duty.

Bob Witty is on a mission to implement a program already proven to reduce firearm-related veteran suicides by 50% in the first year of civilian life. Be an advocate. A copy of the early adopter program is available. Reach out to him, please: bobwitty@icloud.com

CARETAKER FOR GRANDMA JOAN... CHEF JILL SULLIVAN

"The candy lady"

Caretaker: the cook, housekeeper, errand runner, therapist, nurse, listening ear, friend and daughter.

In this chapter I hope to give some insight on what it's like to be the caretaker for an elderly parent. There's a lot of joy in caregiving.

Don't be afraid to laugh, but know that you are also going to cry, too.

MOST IMPORTANTLY~
"Self-care is a priority not a luxury."
Take care of yourself, too.
"You cannot fill another's cup when your cup is empty."

My mom, Grandma Joan.

Everyone loves Grandma Joan. She's one of the sweetest grandmas on the planet, literally. When you go to Grandma Joan's house, the first thing you will see sitting on the living room table is a huge bowl of candy. Paying great attention to the kind of candy everyone loves, she only buys the good stuff. She never misses sending a birthday or holiday greeting card, and you will always find a $20 dollar bill inside.
(Gift giving is her love language)

(But)
On the other side of that coin
She can also be ornery, demanding and short-tempered.
With little or no hesitation, she'll tell you what she thinks.

I'm sorry if someday you end up being her waitress at a restaurant because...
The food is always too cold, the meat is always too tough, and for your sake, I hope the coffee is fresh! That's when I feel like crawling under the table and hiding. It's a running joke at our house: "Is the coffee fresh?" LOL

The onset of Alzheimer's and dementia in the elderly causes frustration, memory loss, agitation and impatience. They have lost a lot of their independence and can take the frustration out on the ones around them. And.... since you're the one with them the most, you will get the brunt of it.

It's important to show parents respect. This might look different for everyone, but we should always try to love and care for those who cared for us first.

Put a little humor and a lot of patience in your back pocket before leaving the house. You're going to need it. Humor in everyday situations is crucial. It can change the dynamic of each awkward interaction. Laugh a little! It's good for the soul - both young and old.

They say laughter is the best medicine, I really do believe that. It's what will get us through.

We knew the time would come when we would have to nominate a caretaker. There's really no way to prepare for that day. It feels like a coin toss, whoever has the most available time wins the caretaker position. Or maybe, whoever pulls the short straw.... tag you're it.

The need for a caregiver seems to appear out of nowhere. If you think you're going to have plenty of time to plan, *think again.*

With no instruction manual, we do our best to figure it all out. I know. I found myself the main caretaker around two years ago. It fell into my lap when my older sister and her husband (who Grandma Joan lives with), were called to serve a mission for our church and would be gone for a year and a half. My other sister holds a corporate job and lives seven hours away. Obviously, she couldn't do it.

Raising my hand, *I will, I'm happy to.* What a true honor it is to serve the ones who've served you for so long.

My rattled awake moment came one night around 11:00 pm. I had retired to bed around 10:00 p.m., heard a loud thud, then a call for help. *"Jill, Jill, help, help!"* A caretaker's worst nightmare. She had fallen against the shower tile and cut her arm pretty badly. It took almost an hour to get her off the floor. She was visibly shaking and scared. After I stopped the bleeding and calmed her down, I was finally able to get her up onto a chair. It definitely rattled us both. From that moment on, we both knew she needed someone there day and night.

Funny how mom's find "that one thing they need NOW." Endless requests. I need this, have you had a chance to do that, *what are you doing right now?* etc etc. So much love and humor in those nagging requests.

Here, just a few of those humorous requests:
#1 *Did you remember my mints?*

As she unrolls her grocery list a mile long, she says... since you're going to the store, I've made a little list of a few things I need. Her list usually consists of 100 different kinds of candy and a couple of healthy options. LOL

After spending a couple of hours at the store, I finally got home. Reaching into the trunk, I grabbed every bag that I could physically carry. Don't we all do this? Carrying in the 10 bags of groceries and loading them all the way down the 12 stairs to her apartment, I see her sitting comfortably in her recliner.

As I'm putting away the groceries, wiping down the refrigerator as I go, the sweat is now rolling down my brow and into my eyes. I hear her yelling something to me in the background.
Did you remember my mints?
Sorry mom, I can't hear you, what was that?
Repeating herself one more time she screams:
DID...YOU...REMEMBER...TO...BUY...MY...MINTS?

By that time, I had walked over to where she was sitting (tired of yelling) and was standing right by her. Holding up the 10 candy bags, I said, "Yes Mom. I also bought the 10 bags of candy you ordered, too." (sarcasm gets me through)

Oh good, I like to suck on them when my allergies cause nasal drip and make me cough.
(Another TMI descriptive moment) They give a long explanation for everything they do.

I do all the shopping online with delivery now. What a lifesaver.

10 useful caregiving tips:
1- Home delivery everything

2 - Create clear boundaries
3 - Learn to respite - a short period of rest or relief from something difficult
4 - Seek out volunteers
5 - Prevent injuries by making your house handicap accessible
6 - Make a backup plan
7- Get organized
8 - Don't make promises you can't keep
9 - Be realistic about what you can/can't do
10 -Have a family meeting early- go over their last day's requests, how do (they) want to handle their last days?

#2 The silent jab
I can hear her in the kitchen banging dishes around, making sure I hear her.
She yells in a loud frustrated voice, *JILL??? WHERE DID YOU PUT MY PITCHER? I want to make some orange juice but I can't find it anywhere.*
Then in a very low voice, she says under her breath, *Since you've been using my kitchen, I can't find anything anymore.*
(the silent jab)
For the record, I put things back where they go. Walking to the cupboard where she usually keeps it, I find it nicely stashed right where she put it. I open the cupboard door and point "Here it is Mom, right here in the corner. Isn't that where you usually put it?"

She walks toward where I'm pointing and says, *Oh ya, ok.*

If she were one of my kids, this is where I would interject a loud THANK YOU! And a firm, YOU'RE WELCOME.

#3 Never good enough

(Working hard in the garden all day we were starving)
Hey mom, we're going to Del Taco, want anything?

Well, I'm not that hungry, I had a big bowl of Great Grains for breakfast. (she went silent for a minute)

Perhaps she was thinking, 'Hmm, maybe I would like some tacos?'

Ok, get me three tacos, the larger ones, I don't like the small ones. One combo burrito. Is that the one that has chicken in it?

No mom, it's got taco meat and beans.

Oh no...I definitely don't want that one. They always give me diarrhea. (blunt) *Just get me the one with the chicken in it, that always sits on my stomach a little better.*

I think to myself, 'Why is there ALWAYS a long explanation to each menu item?' Haha.

As she's eating, she says, *Now I know why I never go to Del Taco. The tacos are always stale and the burritos always give me diarrhea.* (TMI moment) LOL

Remember, she does this with everything. I knew the complaints would come so I just shook my head and laughed. "OK, Mom!"

I can see my sisters reading this right now, shaking their heads up and down in total agreement, saying 'Yep.'

#3 Accidental parental abuse in the car
As she gets in the car and sits down in her seat, I take the seat belt in my hand and try to wrap it around her to buckle

her in. As I go to plug it in, it accidentally grazes her face, she says, *OUCH!*

I promise you, it wasn't that bad. Looking behind me first, I always make sure no one's walking by. They might think I was serious. With a comical voice and silly face, I say, "Sit down and be quiet old lady, or I'll hit you with it again."

*Oh Jill, you are such a smart a***. Haha

Then we look at each other and burst into laughter. I keep the abuse jokes coming just for extra laughs. I love that we have the same humor. It's twisted humor, but we both find it's more fun to laugh about accidental parent abuse than take anything too seriously.

> "Let us always meet each other with a smile,
> for the smile is the beginning of love."
> Mother Teresa

Approximately 1 in 10 Americans age 60 plus have experienced some form of elder abuse. Some estimates range as high as five million elders abused each year. One study estimated that only one in 24 cases of abuse are reported to authorities. Every year, hundreds of thousands of elders are abused. Abuse can come from anyone including children, nursing home staff, spouses, and family members. About 2/3 of abusers are spouses and children, and about 60% of the abusers
are close family members.

We've all seen an elderly person being abused on T.V., and it makes us sick to our stomachs: The evil caregiver who loses his patience and smacks the old lady so hard that it spins her completely around in her wheelchair. She's now crying and holding her face. Then he proceeds to slap the old man who is lying in bed for not eating his lunch. He slaps him so hard that he almost flies out of bed right along with his lunch tray. Food flying everywhere, he proceeds to pull himself back onto bed. A very sad and sick scenario all caused by the hands of a sick and twisted individual. The caregiver seems to have no idea that there is a hidden camera that has captured every act.

Next thing you know, it's on TV and everyone's watching in disgust. We all say to ourselves, I hope they lock him up and throw away the key. There's a special place in hell for people like him. Pure evil.

The Good Times
Planting flowers, playing scrabble, dancing with her in the living room, rescuing her when she fell in the bathroom, watching sunsets together, sunrise breakfasts on the back porch, watching movie after movie, and laughing about old times.

I remember the first time I saw her; about six months had passed in between visits. She was living alone at that time, and she looked awful. Her lips, and around her lips, were purple; her complexion gray and ashy. She had lost so much weight that I hardly recognized her. Fifty pounds is a lot to lose for anybody. After seeing a cardiologist and finding out that she had AFib, we implemented medications. She's now doing much better. She will never be 100%.

What exactly is AFib?
Symptoms include fatigue, heart palpitations, trouble breathing and dizziness. AFib is one of the most common arrhythmias. Risk factors include high blood pressure, coronary artery disease and obesity. Untreated AFib can lead to a stroke. AFib is a common issue that is expected to

affect about 12.1 million people in the country by 2030. A lot of people live years after being diagnosed with AFib.

Since you're the one with them the most, you get the brunt of it. If you understand this, it makes caring for them a little easier. What they say can pierce your heart and make you cry. It's not them, it's the dementia or Alzheimer's talking; it changes how they think and how they react.

Love them through it.

What a true honor it is to serve the ones who've served you for so long.

"To love and be loved is to feel the sun from both sides."
— David Viscott

To Love and Be Loved
Writers: J. Van Heusen, S. Caun
First and 4th verse

To love -and be loved
That's what life's- all about.
Keeps the stars -coming out
What makes a sad heart sing- the birds take wing
To love -and be loved

To be sheltered -and safe from-the storm
To be cozy- and ever- so warm
And for always- to love
And be loved- by you

"Treat others as you would like to be treated."

When you're in a tough spot with your senior loved one, try to take some time to put yourself in their shoes. Maybe they're avoiding a difficult conversation because they're embarrassed or afraid. Perhaps they are responding with anger to an everyday challenge because of the physical or emotional pain they can't express.

Think about your loved one's wants and needs, then think about what you would want if your roles were reversed. Adopting this mindset can be a helpful way to approach communicating with your loved one, and coming up with strategies for difficult choices and transitions, like giving up driving, or accepting the services of a professional home care company.

> "Love begins at home, and it is not how much we do…
> but how much love we put into that action."
> Mother Teresa

> "People are unrealistic, illogical and self-
> centered. Love them anyway"
> Mother Teresa.

> "Life is short and every moment is precious."
> Gad Saad

> "A life not lived for others is not a life. If you
> can't feed a hundred people, feed just one. I
> can do things you cannot, you can do things I
> cannot; together we can do great things."
> Mother Teresa

I know the time will come when I cry out and say, "I miss you mom. I wish you were here."
But she won't be.
Until that time, I'll savor every moment I get to spend with her.

I dedicate this chapter to my mother, Grandma Joan.
I love her with all of my heart and soul and I will miss her greatly when she's gone.
I feel blessed to have been her caretaker, thus having the opportunity of getting to know her on a deeper level by serving her.
If we give everything we have, that's all that is required of us.

Love you always Mom,
Jill

Chef Jill Sullivan is on a mission to share hope in each new day and that a new world of possibilities is for the taking with each new glorious sunrise. No matter the difficulty or struggles we are all going through, it's possible to come out of it and create a new life, a new you. She is a retired executive chef who enjoys serving others, and sharing her love for nutritious and healthy food. Follow her on LinkedIn: www.linkedin.com/comm/mynetwork/discovery-see-all?usecase=PEOPLE_FOLLOWS&followMember=chef-sully-jill-sullivan

THE UNIVERSE'S STORYTELLER...
DOUG THOMPSON

There is no way this is going to become the rest of my life. That is what I *wish* I had told myself as I sat in the office after my annual performance review. Instead, I sat there like a chicken watching television trying to figure out how I was going to support my family without that job. It was not like I was a 30-year-old developer with mad in-demand coding skills. I was slightly younger than the crypt keeper and my only skills were explaining technology to ordinary people without what I call "techsplaining." While this was technically the rattled awake moment, (of course, it's a technicality, I am a nerd), in reality it was the universe telling me I was meant for bigger things. It closed a door to a room where I had been quite comfortable for way too long, and opened a window to show me the stages I was meant to be on.

To understand how we got to the fateful day above, we need to turn on the time machine to replay a couple key moments of the journey that can connect the dots in a way that only a rear-view mirror can. You'll notice that as I tell the tale I do my best to not share the companies involved. The main reason I have done this is that the names of the characters aren't important to the story. If it makes you feel better, substitute Elmer Fudd and Acme Corp. I have spent most of my career working in the tech space and at large multinational corporations, and have made many friends along the way. Most of them worked at multiple companies and their stories all have a similar vibe as the one I tell here. Corporations by nature are not living beings with a soul or heart and therefore tend to make cold decisions. That said, I have learned many things and made a good living working at some of the biggest corporations in the world. Rather than trash them, I used them here as the setting where the protagonist's (AKA Me) journey takes place. Now that all the disclaimers have been told, let us queue for the flashback music and rewind about two years, to the arrival of a new manager.

The announcement of the new manager was made with the customary flair. 'Please welcome "insert the antagonist's name here." He has a long history here and successfully managed the banana hammock group before landing here.' Blah Blah Blah. I immediately searched LinkedIn and surprisingly found he had no social media presence. There were a few company press announcements on the web but not even a LinkedIn profile. What kind of executive does not at least have a LinkedIn page that is nothing more than a resume? This was my first clue that things were going to be different, and not in a good way. Jettisoning my public search, I looked at my Rolodex, (yes, I am THAT old), for internal contacts at groups he previously led. Luckily, I found an old contact from my very first team at the company, and while she did not directly work for this person, she once worked in the same organization. So, I asked her what she knew. She told me that the new manager was extremely focused on their direct reports' success and was a good manager and was well-respected by their teams. Well, if that was all the info I had to go on I would have to trust her perspective, but the lack of a social presence at this time still bugged me; this is not normal.

It was two months before the new manager held a team meeting with no other communication. I was beginning to feel a bit like Harry Potter in the Order of the Phoenix where he had no communication from any of his friends or his leader Dumbledore. Oddly, none of the other team members I worked with every day had heard anything, either. The meeting was OK, and the manager said he would be setting up individual meetings to get to know us better in the next week. The day arose for my meeting, and I was looking forward to learning a bit more about the new manager so I could figure out the best way to deliver for them. That is one thing that you must learn in the corporate world: how to manage up. Those who don't learn how to do this do not stay around long. Fortunately, I had become great at it. Unfortunately, the meeting turned into more of an FBI interrogation with him asking the questions while taking copious notes during my answers. I was clear to point out that I had the best role in the company and that I would like to have him be my last manager. Little did I know that this would be one of those be careful what you ask for moments. As it turned-out, we were on different time schedules. Shortly after my meeting, I scheduled a one-on-one with my manager's manager who was also my key sponsor in this organization. I was assured by my sponsor that I would do well with the new manager which took me from DEFCON 2 back to 4: I was still vigilant but not in a full-on panic. If you ever saw the movie War Games, you would know that DEFCON stands for Defense Readiness Condition; when it gets to zero the nukes are flying, or, in this case, your time there is over.

Up until this point I had proven myself to a couple great sponsors throughout my career, another key to longevity at a corporation. The sponsor needs to be someone in the food chain above your manager; someone who knows your value and that you can deliver. They will be your advocate for new opportunities but also at the annual review time where the "people discussions" happen. This is part of the annual performance review process where promotions and bonus discussions were had, and if you did not have representation here it was usually problematic. So as long as I had my sponsor, I should be fine.

Not long after that meeting, my sponsor took a leave of absence to take care of a family matter with no ETA for return. This was the second sign that the universe was letting me know that I needed to change. Being more afraid of what was possible on the outside, I instead went to DEFCON 3 trying to figure out how I was not going to get voted off the island.

One thing about the universe is that it is persistent. Seeing that I was hunkered down to stay, it gave me a project from the organization's VP. I was to work with our largest customer to come up with a system to measure the customer's state of cyber readiness. Little did I know it at the time, but I was about to experience the business equivalent of Star Trek's Kobayashi Maru. This is designed to test characters in a no-win scenario. To add a little more fuel to the fire, the "people discussions" were on the horizon. It was more important than ever to deliver for my manager as I did not have the air cover of my sponsor.

At first, I thought this was a straightforward problem to solve. We had just introduced some new tools and metrics to measure cybersecurity readiness, so I met with my customer and started gathering their vision. My optimism quickly began to fade after this meeting just realizing what they wanted; specifically, how the constraints they put on what success looked like was not going to be possible. I explored several different possibilities for the next few months only to hear the universe heckling in the background. Think of the scene from "A League of Their Own" where Stillwell, the son of one of the players, was taunting Tom Hanks' character, "You're going to lose. You're going to lose!" That was the Universe taunting me and I did not dare to throw my glove at that little creep. I finally met with the customer and reviewed all the options and we agreed that there was no way at the time to do what he had hoped for, but we would keep an eye on it for future possibilities. I did what was right for the customer but did not deliver for my manager or the VP. During this time, my manager had taken time off to care for their mother who was in hospice, and later passed away. So here I am at the performance discussion, and I had no one to advocate for me. (I don't think my manager would have been much of an advocate for me as we never really jived. To this day he is an enigma.) Back to DEFCON 2.

That brings us back to the beginning of this story. Time for the annual rectal exam, er performance review. I always hated these things because I am horrible about self-reflection of what I do well. Self-promotion didn't jive with my humbleness firewall, but I had been doing these for almost 20 years at this company, and with the sponsor and manager aircover, it had been enough. My manager was back and took on the role of Pontius Pilot delivering the dictate from the crowd, deftly-played by the organization's leadership. I don't think he took any joy in delivering the message, but there was little emotion at all. The message was that I had not delivered on all of my commitments from the first of the year and that I was not getting any bonus and that I was on probation. In reality, the only commitment I had missed was the Kobayashi Maru mentioned earlier. While I had reached a resolution and communicated the results, I didn't deliver what the VP had wanted. I blew out my quota which is normally the make-or-break metric for sales, but that didn't matter. None of my many past awards, recognitions and successes counted for anything. He told me that I had two options: Quit or try to dig myself out. I asked if he knew of anyone who had come back from that scarlet letter, and he said he knew of one. I had a couple of days to decide what my choice would be. Enter DEFCON 1 and the rattled awake moment.

After discussions with my wife and family, and, being someone who did not want to go out on a loss, I decided to stay. I would also be looking hard at opportunities on the outside. I started working on a recovery plan with my manager and had regular check in to measure progress. I was not going to be surprised again. More importantly, I also took time to reflect on what did I really wanted to do with the balance of my career. I looked back to find what I did well. I looked at all those corporate training exercises like Meyers Briggs and Clifton Strengths. What did they tell me about my personality, what my strengths were, and what gave me energy? That last part was the most influential on my next several decisions. I needed to build a runway so that when corporate life ended, I had a way to take off rather than pulling the ripcord on the parachute at twenty thousand feet.

I embraced the signal the universe was sending me that I had been too busy just surviving to recognize. I thought back to when I joined this company, what were the things that made them hire me? Flashback to 20 years where I was working some gigs for them as a side hustle. (This was before the phrase side hustle became popular.) The gig was a country-wide roadshow evangelizing some new products to their huge reseller base. We had a weeklong audition. I got a call back from the leader who said I was the best one there, that I would do half of the 20 events, and would be the lead presenter on all but the first one, where I played second fiddle to him. There were hundreds of people in the audience at each location and when I was on stage, I was invincible. This was my first large-scale experience as a storyteller, and it was AWESOME, and I was good at it.

There were other times in my career that I was able to do more events as part of my job, got even better, and still got the same feeling. I never stopped to consider what made me good at it until we were interviewing candidates for another role like mine on the team. This was with the earlier manager whom I had worked with in two organizations, so we knew each other well. We went through fifteen candidates, at least 10 presentations, and even though they were technically sound, my manager didn't hire any of them. She finally admitted that she was looking for someone who could tell a story like me. She wanted someone who solved a business problem with a story that didn't focus on technology but rather, a personalized story of how they could realize their dreams by doing business with us.

I was honored and yet confused. I didn't think what I did was remarkable, and it wasn't something I consciously focused on, yet it did ring true with my past experiences on stage. Plato said, "Those who tell stories rule society."

Unfortunately, we see too many politicians and leaders telling stories that are not true, but they are ruling society. Ah, but that is a tirade for another time.

However, my story was I didn't have a story: outside of our company's technology, I didn't have a compelling story myself. After all, I had not overcome drug abuse, an abusive relationship, or near-death experiences. I was a normal kid who was an average student and didn't excel at sports. In fact, I was a kid with asthma, my father died when I was in high school, and didn't really have a goal in life. I just took jobs that I liked and did them until I didn't or was forced to change. Who the hell wants to read that book? (Present company excluded.)

While still working to keep the wheels on at the day job, I was engaging on LinkedIn, where I wanted to be a bigger contributor. That is how I came across a co-author of this book, Brian Schulman. He seemed bigger than life but, was telling stories that helped others tap into their potential, so I reached out to him and scheduled some time with him for help. I was still struggling with imposter syndrome and hoped he might be able to help me find what my story was. As you will read or have read, Brian is the nicest person you will ever meet and after just an hour he helped me see that I have several different stories. I have father/grandfather stories, athlete stories (2-time Ironman Finisher), and professional stories, including being a US Patent Holder. Most importantly, I could relate to people in stories. Because these things all happened to me, I did not see that they were remarkable in any way until Brian pointed them out. He inspired me to do a TEDx talk. If I was going to be a keynote speaker, what better way of proving I could do it than that. The talk is an entire chapter itself, but I did learn a lot! I also started my own podcast, which now has over 100 episodes. I wanted to interview great storytellers and learn how to improve my skills. To date, I have also been a guest on more than 20 other podcasts where I get to share my storytelling message.

Back to the grind: as things at the day job progressed, I was making some progress at digging out of the hole. I continued to spend free time looking for signs from the universe by learning about the brain science of stories. I enrolled in mindset classes, met influencers, and made many great connections. I was finding things that gave me energy and feeling more in control of my life. I was always looking for the next sign. Then one day a job alert came up on LinkedIn and as I read the description, it read like it was written for me. It was at a much smaller tech company, but I knew that the universe had brought it to my attention. Things were happening positively, so I moved down to DEFCON 3.

As luck would have it, a former co-worker worked there, so I reached out to her to find out more. She spoke very highly about the company, and sent my resume to the recruiter. Two weeks later I had a screen interview, then a technical panel and a meeting with the hiring manager. Finally, I had to do a presentation/demo for them. They gave me access to their test environment and a case study upon which to base the 20-minute presentation. I had a week to do it. All of a sudden, the imposter meter jumped to 10. For 20 years, I'd been in a different ecosystem, and had never heard of their product before this time. All I had was their documentation site and my ability to learn. I made the most of the week and delivered my demo. My recruiter later said I did one of the best jobs they had seen, and moved to the offer stage. Moving to DEFCON 4, things were looking good for a different future. Enter COVID. They pulled to the job request and my day-job exit ramp closed. Back to DEFCON 2.

Since I was already remote, the isolation didn't bother me much, but my customers were hit hard. I was able to work with a few of them on solutions that enabled a more efficient working environment. It helped me feel good, but all I was getting from my manager was non-committable feedback on my progress. Furthermore, they were cutting heads inside the company, and the jobs on the outside started drying-up, as well. I could feel the storm clouds gathering and expected that DEFCON 0 was imminent.

The universe often works in mysterious ways. It was an early morning call on a Monday that set things in motion. The number looked familiar, but I didn't have a name associated with it. Since there is rarely good news early on a Monday, I almost sent it to voicemail, but a little voice told me to pick it up. It was the recruiter from before telling me they ramped up hiring. She had me at the top of her list, and if I was still interested in the job, all I had to do was to talk to the new VP. I gladly took that call, and an offer came a week later. The package was more of a lateral move than a step up. If that had happened several months back, before the pause, I may not have taken it, preferring to stay with what I knew. That knowledge included confidence that I could work myself out of yet another mess. I think the universe knew this, and put me through all the other things to rattle me awake again so I would gladly take this offer and exit stage right.

While I still work at a corporation, this one is a better fit for the me of today. I get to host the company podcast, have written and been quoted in many articles, spoken on many stages, and I have grown. I have reinvented myself, so I stay relevant. While I don't plan on staying here for 20 years, I plan on staying as long as I am having fun, growing, and making an impact.

I hope you see yourself in the story as the protagonist who is just living life not really paying attention to the universal signals around you until there is a business change, perhaps it is AI, and your future looks cloudy. You may go through some cloudy times where you doubt yourself and your skills and you want to hold onto what is familiar, feeling reluctant to embrace new things. You may have a single moment that changes everything, or, like my story, where life is a puzzle, and you have that one moment that is the missing piece; the one that clarifies everything and rattles you awake. When this happens, you have two choices: hunker down and hope it passes, or be mindful of all the opportunities around you that call to your soul. I missed many of them along the way but since I have been awake, I have seen so many of them. Some are scary, yet they can easily be turned into excitement with the right attitude. Instead of letting the corporation put me out to pasture because I lost my why, I have followed it to greener pastures where I can share it with those who need to hear it. Often the fight is not what you think, and the quote below should give you faith.

"You may encounter many defeats, but you must not be defeated. In fact, it may be necessary to encounter the defeats, so you can know who you are, what you can rise from, how you can still come out of it." – Maya Angelou

The rattled awake moment helped me find my why: to tell stories like this one; stories that help others find and share their stories. LinkedIn is a wonderful place where I have engaged with many of the people in this book. Opportunities come from those engagements if you get out there and tell your stories. I would love to share this with you or your company on stage or at an event. I'm easy to find as I am TheDougThompson.

Doug Thompson is on a mission to inspire technology professionals to maximize their success by learning to connect with people through stories. An award-winning sales engineer, dynamic TEDx speaker, MC, and host of multiple podcasts including The Doug Thompson podcast where he shares his storytelling insights to connect with his tribe of fellow storytellers. You can find him on LinkedIn at https://www.linkedin.com/in/thedougthompson/

BECOMING... NANCY DEBRA BARROWS

What does it say about me if the happiest I have been, in a long while, was during a worldwide pandemic? No seriously. The world was a terrifying, unpredictable, chaotic nightmare and I was blissful! I can say that because I didn't experience the worst of the pandemic. My family and friends, while isolated from the outside world, remained healthy physically and mentally (mostly). We were able to gather via virtual platforms like Zoom, Facebook Messenger and LinkedIn LIVE. My job went virtual and remained stable and secure. I know these privileges weren't extended to everyone.

Every day was like the first few moments when you wake up after it has snowed overnight. Peaceful. Quiet. Beautiful. Crazy, right? For someone who is a chronic worrier, I was calm. Somehow, in the midst of the chaos, I found clarity. I discovered happiness.

During the pandemic I was living alone with my two cats. While they didn't always understand the concept of 'social distancing', I never had to fight with them over the remote, what was for dinner, which ice cream flavor to buy or ration toilet paper - there was no debate about how many squares per trip to the potty each person would be allotted.

During the pandemic, I realized how small my world had become. It wasn't distressing. In fact, I leaned into it and found it comforting. Who is this person!?! Leaning in? Free of worry? I want to be this woman when I don't grow up!

One month before the pandemic, I had finally gotten to a place of feeling human again. I remember the day. I remember how odd it felt to feel 'okay' after having been lost and drowning for so long. It was uncomfortable and surreal.

What was I before I was human again...?

A few years prior to the pandemic, during my divorce, my community abandoned me. I experienced a 'mass exodus' of 'friends' from my life. Neither of us had done anything heinous. My ex and I grew apart. It was heart-breaking. People often believe that if you are the one who is asking to end the marriage that it is easy on you. Far from it, for me. It was one of the hardest, most devastating things I have ever done. We had been married for 16 years and dated for 18 months prior to that. Everything in my life had been 'touched' by my ex-husband. It didn't help those friends of 15 years chose sides and nobody chose mine. I'm sure I don't have to tell you that waking up suddenly alone in the world does a number on your head.

I suppose I was the enemy because I was brave enough to say things had changed. WE had changed and I believed that we both deserved to be loved deeply, and fully, by a partner who was also IN love with us.

I was the enemy because my telling my ex-husband that I could no longer be married brought the relationships of those around me into focus. It put them under a microscope. And, people were frightened by what they saw. They fought hard to go back to living blindly, and my marriage ending became uncomfortable for them to be around.

I was the enemy because I refused to speak badly of my husband to anyone who knew both of us. He wasn't a bad guy. He was just no longer the right guy for me to spend the rest of my life with. **His pity card trumped my silence.**

I was the enemy because I was no longer showing up as the same person, in the same ways and their discomfort over all of it spurred them to toss me aside. No, I'm not coming to your seven-year old's birthday party and eating cake across from my soon to be ex-husband and smiling. I was broken, depressed and grieving. Nobody wanted to meet me where I was. They kept demanding that I be someone I wasn't. One of my 'friends' even said to me, "You said this was going to make you happy. Then why aren't you happy?", with such venom. It was a slap in the face. A wake-up call. If I wasn't willing to make them comfortable by changing how I was feeling and acting, there was no room for me in their lives. Thank you, Universe, for making it clear where not to put my energy. For the record, I never said it was going to make me happy. I said it was the right decision. Those are two very different things.

I know I'm not the only person who has a story like mine. You know, the one where the support system, the community and family, that you have shown up for time and time again, ghosts you when your time of need arises. When those you expected to step up, step back.

Have you found yourself alone in a dark and difficult time? Raise your hand if you know what I'm talking about.

After being abandoned by my so-called friends, I decided that I didn't need anyone. Relying on myself was the only safe option moving forward. I could face this, and everything else that came my way, alone. Whatever pain, grief or anguish forging ahead by myself brought was better than the betrayal of people who love you walking away when you need them most. It's not like we had never been through adversity together before. We had banned together and seen one another through illness, the murder of a beloved mother and grandfather, and times of financial uncertainty. I wouldn't be 'fooled' again. Never.

Have you ever wondered, "How did I get here? Is this really my life? How did I end up in the wrong story!?"

I mentioned to my therapist that I felt as if I was experiencing PTSD around making friends. I *was certain* that they had the capacity to, and would, love and support us BOTH through this difficult time. I thought I knew the people in my circle. Turns out, I didn't. I began to mistrust my judgment about people - and I make my living by knowing people. I didn't believe others could be steadfast and non-judgmental. So, my world got small. Really small. Long philosophical conversations with my two cats kinda of small. At the same time, it expanded in ways I could never have fathomed.

Remember, I said the COVID pandemic was the happiest time I've experienced in as long as I can remember? The picture I painted seems at odds with that statement, but it isn't. The isolation it created set the stage for some powerful, transformative moments of growth.

During the pandemic, I spent a lot of time with myself and my story. I was present in ways I hadn't been before. Things slowed down. I felt grounded. It was a 'perfect storm' that created a wave of growth. A convergence of circumstances that paved the way for several significant transformations.

One.
Not searching for the self-care my body and mind needed, I found it. I discovered that my self-care was *doing nothing*! Nobody ever talks about that option! Find a hobby. What's your passion? What fills your cup? I tried getting my hair colored and cut, treating myself to a manicure/pedicure, being in nature; I joined a book club, took knitting classes, attempted exercising, etc., all in an attempt to find the things I could DO to take care of myself.

I used to joke that I'm terrible at being a girl. I don't want to go sit in a salon and get my hair done for hours, or get my nails done. It's not nourishing my soul and being empathic, it's like - nope that's not it! I now know what I need. I need to be home. I need to get into jammies and receive that unconditional love my cats offer; sit on the couch and do nothing. Before the pandemic I was busy running around trying to fill the time. That's what I thought I was supposed to do. Self-care, I believed, was the act of doing *something*.

I needed the gift of nothing! I'm not sure why I was waiting for permission to boldly do nothing, despite knowing it's what my body and mind craved. They told me every day. The fatigue, forgetfulness, irritability, loss of interest in things I used to love, headaches... Hellloooo! Why didn't I see it sooner? Have you been there? In that ah-ha moment? The one where you have to take a breath and forgive yourself for not seeing what you can now see so clearly? Yeah, me neither, (but make sure you forgive yourself. You can't know, until you know.)

Two.

I spent time with my story in ways I hadn't before. I got to see and know it differently, which helped me see and know myself differently. I stepped fully into having gratitude for EVERYTHING that had happened on my journey. All parts of my story. The good, the bad and the cringeworthy.

Have you ever spent time trying to outrun your past? It is exhausting, right? Mine isn't an easy story for which to be grateful. The abridged version...trauma then some more trauma and add a little more trauma and you are just about there. Sexual abuse, anorexia, an unidentified learning disability & undiagnosed ADD, confronting my abuser, dropping out of college, major depressive episodes. It was ugly, snotty and unsexy to say the least. For a good part of my life, I felt I was broken beyond repair. Tell me, how does one find gratitude for that?

It was impossible, until I finally took off my mask and became 100% committed to being 100% me, 100% of the time. That's when the amazing happened. I met the real Nancy Debra Barrows, and I liked her. Like, *really* liked her. You know that moment when you are reading a book or watching a movie and you figure out it was Mrs. White, in the conservatory with the candlestick? It was kinda like that. I realized that in order to be the person I was, I had to go through everything leading up to it. If I had skipped even one thing, I don't know who I would be. Not only did I like myself, I was proud of the ways I could show up and help others *because* of my experiences.

I'm going to ask you to pause here. Use the margins or inside covers of this book. If you prefer, take notes on your phone. They all work. Now, grab something with which you can write and make a list of all the people you are 100% authentic with. Then come back.

Look at your list. Is your name on it? Before the pandemic, my name wouldn't have appeared on my list, but it is crucial that it does. It is the first step in showing up for yourself and #RadiatingReal! You deserve the unconditional love and acceptance that follows.

Three.
I discovered LinkedIn. While my relationship with my cats was thriving, a friend insisted that there was more to life and 'forced' me to explore LinkedIn. She had been on the platform for years and had told me many stories of the connections she made and the community she had built. *Oh, That's nice.* "No thanks! I'll pass". However, she wouldn't take no for an answer.

She posted a video of her and I that we had filmed a year prior. In the video we discussed our personal struggles with mental health and our fears around people knowing who we were in our darkest moments. Yes, tequila was involved. I knew she intended to post it on LinkedIn. That was fine by me. I never planned on being on LinkedIn and I certainly wouldn't be meeting anyone who had seen it. Famous last words. She posted the video on LinkedIn and tagged me. She then started sending me screenshots of what people were saying. The support they were offering and the unconditional love they were flowing, to me, a perfect stranger. I was now a LinkedIn user! Does it sound silly or insincere to say that LinkedIn changed my life? Well, it did. I discovered a community I didn't know I needed and a family I didn't know I had. When I speak on stage, I always ask for a show of hands, of "who thinks it is acceptable to talk about sexual abuse on LinkedIn?". People try their best to melt into their seats and I worry that someone, someday, will sustain a neck injury from shaking their head "no" so vigorously! But that is exactly what I did. I didn't know about an algorithm. I didn't know there were do's and don'ts. I showed up as myself and shared my story.

I found my passion and my purpose & 10 months later, I was named one of the Top 50 Most Impactful People of LinkedIn, out of nearly billion users. What the what?!? Me??? I was new to the platform. What extraordinary thing had I done? I showed up. I had been genuine, authentic and that was inspiring to others. The birth of another ah-ha moment…being me is a skill. Everything flowed from being me? Huh. Being me IS a skill! Showing up and #RadiatingReal to sharing the ugly, snotty, unsexy parts of living life and being human. That's what I had done.

Four.
I *embraced* that being me is a skill. Do you consider being who you are a skill? If you said anything other than, "It is!", not to worry. We each discover it in our time. In our way. You are here, reading this, which means you already have taken the first step. Congratulations! Being me is influential, inspiring and sought-after. It took me nearly two years to understand and accept this fact. I had inherent value. I was finally ready to own that. For so long, because I hadn't had years of higher education in studying how to be me, I dismissed that value. If I went to school for years to be a doctor or engineer or a trade school to become a highly skilled plumber or hair stylist, I would monetize that skill unapologetically. That ability. That expertise. And, I would have no problem being paid what I was worth. People would be paying me top dollar without question.

Showing up as me being me sharing my story. That was it. Too simple to be true, but it is. That's what earned me keynote stages. It's what earned me invites to books. It's what earned me coaching clients. It is what earned me awards and accolades. It was me.

It was solely me. I didn't go to college for it, but I *had* been schooled, through my *experience* - the school of life. People pay me for my skill, my wealth of expertise and the years of experience it took to gain it. By the way, monetize is not a four-letter word!

Take a moment and make a list of your best qualities and the things at which you excel. Everything you think, put it on the list. Then, make a list of the things you consider to be your worst qualities or shortfalls. Again, if it pops into your head, write it down. Do both without judgment. Nobody is checking your list, so be honest.

How challenging was that? Which list was harder to create? For most people, it is identifying the best in ourselves. Think about that. How could one possibly think of being themselves as a skill, if they don't identify with the greatness they possess. One more step. Email three people who love you unconditionally, whom you value. Email them (email - this is something you want to hold on to and refer back to. Trust me on this one.) and ask, "What do you love about me? What would you say are my best qualities and the things I'm good at?". Seeing ourselves through someone else's eyes is a gift. To have who you are and how you are received reflected back to you is powerful! I don't know about you, but I long ago accepted that I'm not smarter than everyone I know. Which means, if several people are saying it, even if I don't see or believe it, I need to trust that it is true. These emails will become your "North Star" for when you forget who you are and what a difference you make in this world!

Showing up as your truest self is more powerful than we give ourselves credit for. There is a story within each of us, a voice that can positively impact the life of another human in an important way. Being you IS a skill.

I teach people how to tap into the power of LinkedIn by #RadiatingReal and sharing personal content (there is a difference between personal and private. We are all entitled to our 'secrets'.) I hear what people don't say. I comfortably go to the darkest places with another human being and allow them to simply be - but not do it alone. I inspire people to step out of their comfort zones and show up for themselves. I partner with people to clear the clutter of the inherited beliefs that we all carry. I journey with them as they take off their masks, find their authentic inner voice and get comfortable using it. I help people discover the power of being them - the skill of who they are and what they bring to the table. And, I stand with them when they harness the power of sharing their authentic selves with the world. It is an honor and privilege. When on stage, I have been gifted with a powerful 'voice' within and the ability to make everyone present feel seen, heard, loved and valued. Whatever value I provide to others, they provide more to me.

The pandemic was a time of growth and discovery for me. It gave me the time and space to find the ME I didn't know was there. And then, the pandemic 'ended'.

Five.
I had to return to living a 3D life. My presence in the world was, once again, required. Don't get me wrong, I was immensely grateful that lives weren't being lost in the

horrific numbers that they had been, but I didn't appreciate the consequence of things going back to the way they were 'pre-pandemic'. NO!!!! I had finally found my center. I was happy! I was thriving! I didn't want to get resituated, reacclimated, returned to where I was before! I didn't want to go through re-entry. Every day that that reality drew closer, I felt my anxiety grow and my mood darken. How was I going to hold on to this happiness? I know I'm not alone here. And, I know I'm not alone in being hesitant to admit that I dreaded returning to 'life as we knew it' before COVID.

So how did I do it? Frightened and skeptical. Mindfully and remaining vigilant. That's how I did it. We are powerful even when we are experiencing doubt and are afraid. I leaned into that community I mentioned. I leaned into the lessons learned and refused to hide myself or make myself small. I trusted that I could, and would, show up for myself and for others. I continued to show up as me, help others and in return, my soul was fed and my heart remained full. Remember, it is ok to 'do' as long as we are intentional and remain aware of what the "doing" costs/ credits us. Remember, the true you is beautiful and worth fighting to discover and fiercely protect.

Just as I did, you can navigate the challenges and changes that life presents. You can continue to shine your light, to inspire others, and to be a force for positive change.

In the midst of chaos, I found clarity. In the heart of isolation, I discovered happiness. The pandemic, with all its uncertainty and fear, offered me a gift – the opportunity to truly see myself, to embrace my story, and to find my authentic self.

Show up as yourself, unapologetically. Embrace the skill of being you, and let your authentic self-radiate out into the world. In doing so, you not only honor your own journey but also inspire those around you to do the same. We are all powerful beings, and together, we can shape a world filled with authenticity, love, and acceptance. And as we step back into the world, let us remember that our power lies not just in what we do, but in who we are. It's a skill worth celebrating, a journey worth embracing. So, let us continue to show up, to be authentic, and to radiate our real selves, for that is where our true strength lies.

Lean into your community, embrace the lessons you've learned, and trust yourself to show up as your true self. Just as I did, you can navigate the challenges and changes that life presents. You can continue to shine your light, to inspire others, and to be a force for positive change.

Let's go beyond surviving to thriving in this journey called life. Embrace the power of being you, and watch as your story transforms into a beacon of hope and inspiration for others. The world needs your unique light, now more than ever. In an ever-changing world that presents unrealistic expectations for what "real" is and has taught us that you are strong if you can muscle through, we have the tools to change this narrative.

Life has a way of throwing us into the depths of uncertainty and despair, but it also has a way of revealing our strength and resilience. We may be bruised and weathered along the way, but by becoming, we transcend. My hope is that you have found something in my story that resonates with your own. That you feel empowered to take one step forward, followed by another and another and another.

I want to leave you today with something that speaks to the process of becoming and the beauty that is revealed when you are real.

"Does it hurt?" asked the Rabbit.
"Sometimes," said the Skin Horse, for he was always truthful. "When you are Real you don't mind being hurt."

"Does it happen all at once, like being wound
up," he asked, "or bit by bit?"

"It doesn't happen all at once," said the Skin Horse.
"You become. It takes a long time. That's why it doesn't happen often to people who break easily, or have sharp edges, or who have to be carefully kept."

"Generally, by the time you are Real, most of your hair has been loved off, and your eyes drop out and you get loose in the joints and very shabby. But these things don't matter at all, because once you are Real you can't be ugly, except to people who don't understand."

Excerpt from the Velveteen Rabbit By: Margery Williams

Nancy Debra Barrows is on a mission to transform hearts and lives with her profoundly moving and inspiring keynote (addresses/presentations/speaking.) She has empowered countless people to embrace their unique selves through her 'Chick With the Toolbelt' coaching programs. Nancy Debra uses her remarkable gift of connecting with people in a way that's deeply authentic and incredibly engaging to help individuals and teams uncover their true potential and overcome obstacles, whether they are personal or career-related. Known as the Queen of Engagement, she has been recognized by Linkedin as a 4X Top Voice in Personal Branding, Personal Coaching, Public Speaking & Communication, named one of the Top 50 Most Impactful People, one of the Top 50 Most Inspired Connections, one of the Top 250 Risings Stars & Influencers to Watch, is a 2X Best-Selling Author, Keynote Speaker, Founder & Chief Excitement officer of The Chick With The Toolbelt, a dedicated cat mama, lover of cheesecake and a native New Yorker. Connect with her here:

https://www.linkedin.com/in/nancybarrows

FROM APATHY TO ACTION...
GENE PETRINO

Unleashing the Warrior Within

What the fuck just happened to me! I have always been patient, but this kid's words ignited a fuse that obliterated everything. The fact is that there have only been a couple of occasions in all of my life that I felt such violent rage. This time was definitely different. His words unleashed an anger so fierce that I stopped in my tracks. I could barely ask the questions I needed to help this poor child. Luckily, his smile, through his tears, brought me back. At least a little.

Let me go back to the beginning. I had been a police officer for about 11 years at that point. I was salty. Though I figured it all out and really believed I'd seen everything. The early years of my career were all piss and vinegar. I wanted to save the world. I was that "guy." I was so idealistic that it could make you puke. However, life had beaten that out of me by my sixth or seventh year on the job. I had been abused by the public just because I held them accountable. Sometimes physical, most of the time verbal. I mastered the art of detachment.

Do you remember the beer commercial where the NFL coach yelled at the referee, and he just stood there with a blank expression. The announcers asked where he learned to take the abuse, and then they showed a picture of him at home with his wife yelling at him. That was me. I had been cursed out by the best of them and had incredibly thick skin. That's one reason I was caught off guard by a 9-year-old boy's story. I'll get to that in a minute.

It wasn't just the public. When I started my job, it was normal for a supervisor to eviscerate you in front of your peers. It was like a cruel game designed to make you stronger, or just because the supervisors had no personality and were just being dicks. I remember when I asked to have a bulletproof vest issued to me and was asked why I wanted one. My answer was straightforward, so I replied, "I don't want to get shot." I could feel the outpouring of love from the captain as he said in a severe and uncaring voice, "You get paid to get shot." I'm not the most intelligent guy, but I don't remember reading that in the job description. It must have been the fine print.

Anyway, I had settled into a work-life of apathy. Don't get me wrong. I was always on time, rarely called out sick, and responded to every call I was dispatched to. I just did the bare minimum. It's what they wanted. Supervisors back then only wanted to get through the shift without any injuries or serious issues. Before we went in service, most briefings ended with "Don't get me sued" or "Stay off the radio unless you're called."

Proactive law enforcement was not only something you wouldn't get rewarded for; you would actually get punished. They were creative back then. I remember one time I had to count the number of stop signs in the district. All because I stopped to talk to a citizen who flagged me down to tell me he thought his neighbor had died because thousands of flies covered the window of his neighbor's house. What actually happened was that the neighbor moved out, leaving meat in the refrigerator that rotted when the power was turned off. It was gross but not the worst I'd seen or smelled.

So, back to my story. I started the day just like every day. Filled with a sense of dread and sarcasm. I went to the morning briefing and saw we were short-staffed again. Once that was over, I immediately drove to a convenience store to get my coffee. I braced myself for another agonizing day in a job I had grown to hate.

This day was made even better because it started to rain. Now, in South Florida, we get some pretty severe rain. The drops were the size of marbles and were ice cold. I'm from Florida, so maybe not as freezing as some might think, but it was cold nonetheless.

My goal for the day was to go home dry and uninjured. I began to drive through my assigned zone. Overall, it was a great zone to work, except for one area near a high school. It was notorious for all types of street-level crimes. Burglary, robbery, narcotics, domestic violence, stolen cars, and a slew of juvenile complaints. Was I going to be spared the usual headaches because of the rain? It was peaceful as I drove slowly, sipping my hot coffee and listening to the rain hit the roof of my car. Maybe the job wasn't that bad.

As if that thought were magic, the rain stopped. I felt God was about to play another of his famous jokes on me, and I was right.

I turned down the most notorious streets in the zone, and I could make out the shape of a small boy standing on the sidewalk. He wasn't walking to school; he was just standing there. As I got closer, I saw he was soaked, but his face looked particularly wet. It wasn't from the rain. It was from tears.

I pulled up to him and got out of my car. He wouldn't look directly at me, and I realized he might be autistic. I turned my radio down and approached him slowly. He had been through enough, and I didn't want to cause a sensory overload.

He told me he was walking to school when an older boy stole his umbrella. While that didn't seem like the worst thing in the world to me, to him, it was. I quickly learned that he was an avid lover of soccer. It was apparent as soon as he began to describe his umbrella. He carefully explained that the handle had a small soccer ball at the base that helped him hold on to it when it was windy. The canopy was designed to look like a soccer ball. He said he pretended to be inside a soccer ball when he looked up through it. His smile was infectious as he described it. This was his prized possession.

But that's when it happened. It felt like I was hit by a truck. My adrenaline flooded my system. That turned to rage. Who could do this to a small child, let alone one with special needs? What has our world become?

Usually, I would just take the report and maybe drive around looking for a suspect if I was bored. This was different. I was out for blood. I wanted to make the "person" who did this pay. I decided to stop at nothing to reunite that boy with this beloved umbrella. This was war.

I spent the next two days tracking down the degenerate who had committed this crime. My newfound proactivity caught the eyes of my co-workers. I was at the receiving end of many jokes about me trying to "save the world." That didn't deter me. Even my closest friends were confused by my awakened determination but supported my efforts. To my delight, and with their help, I was successful. I identified the suspect, arrested him, and recovered the umbrella. Eventually, returning it to the little boy.

Now, this is where my life changed. I was proud of being able to help someone. I felt a new sense of pride and purpose. After some weighty introspection, I realized that I had become what I always disliked. I was a victim and didn't even realize it.

I blamed the poor working conditions, abusive treatment by supervisors and the public, and anything else I could identify as why I was filled with such discontent. The truth is, it was all my fault. My attitude was garbage. You can't control what life throws at you, but you can control how you react.

I accepted the fact that my attitude drives my satisfaction in life. I reconnected with the reason I started a career in law enforcement. I wanted to help people, not be victims and protect those who could not help themselves.

I declared war on crime in my zone. After one month, I began getting noticed in my agency. After two months, I began to get support from my agency. In the end, I was able to turn the entire area around. I made a significant impact on the crimes in the area. I was greeted with love and support from the residents who had been suffering. It was the closest I had ever come to making a difference that mattered.

My attitude change also impacted the direction of my career. I was suddenly sent to specialized training and given special assignments to reduce crime. By this point in my career, we had a new Police Chief. This man was a true leader. He immediately put the officer's safety and care at the top of his priorities. Morale had changed. Proactive law enforcement was encouraged. The fact is that we had never felt support like this one man gave. To this day, I would follow him into hell and back if he asked.

The remaining years of my career were filled with exciting assignments. Some of those assignments included being the Street Crimes Unit Supervisor, part of a multi-agency gang task force, and the coup de grâce, SWAT Commander.

So, this all led me to where I am today. You see, one of my duties as the SWAT Commander was to teach organizations in our city how to respond to active shooter incidents. Our course was in such high demand that it prevented me from doing my regular job. As such, we had to turn many organizations away. This is where my company was born. I had tactical training and real-world experience when I led my team during the active shooter incident at the Fort Lauderdale Airport in 2017.

We started Survival Response with the mission to help people survive unthinkable situations. While we had some success, something was nagging at me. Something was missing. It took me a couple of years to pinpoint it. The issue was that we were not seeing a decrease in active shooter incidents. In fact, they were increasing exponentially. The solution was staring at us in the face. The focus was solely on a reactive approach in teaching how to respond to these horrific incidents instead of how to PREVENT them!

This answer occurred to me shortly after my retirement in 2020. It was right after the lockdowns from COVID.

All of our corporate clients canceled because no one was working. I used the time to my advantage and finished my master's degree.

This led me to understand the deeper issues regarding violent attacks. Specifically, workplace violence. I started pulling at the thread of academic studies and once again found that familiar rage bubbling up inside me. Study after study kept pointing at the epidemic of workplace violence in our healthcare system. The most disturbing was that over 75% of all workplace violence occurs in healthcare. How is that possible?

The problem was more profound and more personal to me than I could have imagined. With every pull of the thread, I could feel a connection with the experience of healthcare workers. This became evident as soon as I started talking to them. I conducted over 1,500 interviews with these workers whose stories showed the themes that mimicked my early days in law enforcement. Tyrannical treatment by the administration, horrible working conditions, short staffing, low morale, and physical and verbal abuse by patients and family members were all the souvenirs I collected throughout my career.

So, I found myself facing a problem I was compelled to address. I again declared war. This time, I wanted to help those who dedicated their lives to helping others. Armed with my personal experience, academic research, and witness accounts of those suffering, I was ready to create a system of change.

Addressing the epidemic of violence is my mission. It is an uphill battle, but one that needs to be addressed. For those in healthcare now, I want you to know that we see you. Often, the silent support for those in the service professions is unrecognized. But trust me, we've got your backs.

I want you to know that change is coming. New government regulations and a slew of professionals are attacking the issue head-on. I came out the other side of similar circumstances. You will survive. But first, you have to dig deep. Remind yourself of the reasons you went into the profession. Understand that while you can't control things that happen, you can control how you react. I want to rattle awake the warrior inside you so you can be part of the solution. You are strong. You are worthy. You are valued. Let's work together and end this nightmare so you and everyone can benefit from your healing hands.

Gene Petrino is on a mission to empower healthcare workers to go from being victims of violence to being masters at identifying threats before an attack occurs. He is a distinguished security expert with over three decades of exemplary law enforcement and private security service, including a notable tenure as a SWAT Commander. You can find him on LinkedIn": https://www.linkedin.com/in/genepetrino

DADDY ROCKS!...MICHAELA
RIORDAN TURNER, PSYD

Never go into the mind without the body.
Mindfulness is in the body, not the mind.
Mindfulness is an experience, not a behavior.
You can experience mindfulness with a rock.
—Michaela Riordan Turner, PsyD

I taught kindergarten and first grade for most of my teaching career. Being with five- and six-year-olds for seven hours per day over a span of years, taught me how to reduce concepts and instructions to the smallest and most concrete components. Every Tuesday, I introduced the first graders to their dictation sentences using their spelling words from the new unit that was introduced on Monday. Copying the sentences from the board onto their paper helped with their eye-hand coordination, gave them practice in reading, punctuation, and prepared them for the dictation test on Thursday where one sentence was repeated twice, and they wrote it from memory.

Grace raised her hand. When I called on her, she said that she had a question about number four. I asked her to read it out loud. Grace perfectly read: My dog said, "Ruff." The spelling word in that sentence was dog. "What's your question?" I said. She got a worrisome look on her face and hesitated for a moment before she answered. "Um. I don't have a dog." That's okay, I said. You can still write the sentence. Grace was so relieved. That's the concreteness of five- and six-year-old children. Adults have a tendency to forget all about that.

I learned from them and applied that ability to look for the most basic and concrete component of a complex problem in my adult world.

In my doctoral program, I already knew that I was going to write my dissertation about mindfulness, so every paper I wrote over three years had something about mindfulness in it. When I started my dissertation, my committee chairperson stated that I had to write about people; I could not write about mindfulness. Hmmm. My task then was to discover the population around me of which not much was known. I discovered dads, and the topic around which little was known: dads help-seeking.

Dads do not seek help for different reasons than mothers who don't seek help. This is just to point out that there is nothing wrong with dads; quite the contrary. Dads rely on themselves. If dads need help, they will go to a friend or family member. Dads play! That fact was the one silver thread that was woven throughout decades of parse father research. Dads cannot be influenced by authority or intimidated by the state the way mothers have been, but that's a different article.

You've read and heard about the absence of fathers at home being a large contributory factor to school shootings, teen suicide (the second leading cause of death), and cyber bullying.

There are other contributing factors to the father problem. Distractions. Cell phones. YouTube. Instant messaging. Facebook. LinkedIn. "I wish I was a cell phone. Then my dad would pay attention to me." That was a story that made the rounds on social media. Be mindful, they say. Take mindful fathering classes they say; but this is a direct affront to dad's self-image. If dads have to admit there is a problem, that is equivalent to admitting failure; plus mindfulness and its practice are hard work. Who has the time to do that?

Dads are inventing their new roles as they go along. They're looking for the simplest and easiest ways to be mindful; to be the best dads they can possibly be. What if dads did not have to ask for help at all and still received the quintessential guidance that made the most difference in their families—in the length of a nanosecond? The answer is what this story is about, and it exists within the realm of play.

There is a lot of confusion out there about what mindfulness is and is not. What no one has stated, and what this story asserts, is that mindfulness is an experience that can last a nanosecond and occurs inside of a relationship. All you have to do is notice what you see, hear, taste, touch, and smell—in the moment. That information will tell you everything you need to know about your world. When you do that ten times a day, your life will change.

I noticed that the kindergartners needed movement in the morning to fine tune their concentration abilities, so I integrated yoga poses into the classroom one school year. Their favorite pose was the cobra pose. One day, I stepped out of the classroom to speak with another teacher, and when I returned all the children were in the cobra pose. To make it fun, I ran screaming across the classroom and hopped on top of my desk. When they stood up, laughing,

I asked them with a dumbfounded expression and a voice filled with awe, "How did you do that?" They were thrilled that they had fooled me. Their brains learned even better because they were in an environment that recognized them on their level with fun and joy. You can have that fun and joy in your household routines, too.

You want to have relationships with your children, yet, sometimes, there is nothing to talk about. What if there were? What if you talked about a rock that was the focus of a mindfulness game that you and your children invented? What if this mindfulness game was the tether to keep you related; designed to keep the rapport going no matter what the circumstances? Would you want to know about this game?

It's called the hide-and-seek Daddy Rocks mindful fathering game. Here is the premise and how you play. Because everything occurs inside of a relationship, you and your children establish that first by finding two rocks in your yard, or in the park, or next to a creek. Including the children in creating the game has them invested in playing it with you. When you get home, decorate the rocks with the word Daddy and invite your children to add paint, glitter, feathers, whatever you have a mind to use.

When you are finished, place one rock on the shelf for later. With the other rock in your hand, you tell the children that you have invented a hide-and-seek game around the rock. Their brains will light up like a Christmas tree around the word 'game.' Watch their postures lean in. Tell them how to play. This is your element, Dads, because playing is what you do; it's common knowledge.

What you are going to say is that you want the children to hide the 'daddy' rock in a place where you will find it

—in a dresser drawer, in your briefcase, in your shoe, in the kitchen cabinet, in your car; anywhere that you will find it. Tell them that when you see the rock you are going to wake up to what is happening around you, that is to say what you see, hear, taste, touch, and smell; everything that is occurring in the moment. You will do that for the minimum of a nanosecond and for the maximum of your own determination. After you do that, you will replace the rock, in a predetermined location, where your children will see it, so that they can hide the rock again for you to find.

The genius part of the game is that you and your children maintain a rapport around the game even while you travel, while you work long hours, and while you live in different residences. The game becomes a topic of conversation, of something in common. You can talk about what you noticed. Inside of the new relationship you create by simply noticing, you might notice subtle differences in your children's behavior and address them before they become a problem. You might see a furrowed brow, an extra layer of resistance in getting up and going to school, more fighting and pushing than usual. The changes in behavior tell you something, and when you notice, you can sit down with your children and ask what's going on. You forge a new meaning to fathering inside of your family, your routines, and your way of playing the Daddy Rocks game. You are able to add an extra layer of safety to your family.

One dad was the most enthusiastic around the game. He and his teenage son, who had Down's Syndrome, devised their own way of playing the game. The son hid the rock in a place where dad could not find it. Dad looked everywhere and had great difficulty finding the rock every time his son hid it. He even called his son on the telephone when the teen was living at his mother's house that week to ask where he had hidden the rock. The son wouldn't tell. This dad even dreamed about looking for and finding the rock. The teen returned to his dad's house for the week, while dad sat in the dark, watching the NFL game on television. His son placed the Daddy Rock on the coffee table and stated matter of factly, "You couldn't find it, remember?" The dad noticed that his son was using the rock to say, "Look at me, Dad, not the game." The Daddy Rocks game became a subject of conversation when they were driving together, too.

One dad worked from home. He was under pressure to get a project finished before the next morning. His nine-year old son was doing everything in his power to keep his dad's attention on him. Exasperated, the dad firmly told his son that he was going to have to figure out a task by himself, and dad turned around to trudge up the stairs to his office. That was when Dad noticed the rock out of the corner of his eye. At that moment, the dad turned around and gave his son the attention that he was craving.

Are you curious about what you might notice when you play the Daddy Rocks game with your children?

Getting to the basic component of any situation, any relationship, will give you power to influence the environment and provide what the moment calls for. 'Noticing' is the elemental kingdom of kindergarten and 'noticing' is the elemental part of your family. That is exactly what you are going to do while playing the Daddy Rocks game: you are going to notice what is going on around you, through your five senses, when you spy the rock. Mindfulness can be learned and experienced with a rock. There is no "doing mindfulness," there is only *being* mindful, period. Then you notice what you notice. This is the power of playing the Daddy Rocks game. When you see the rock, you notice what you see, hear, taste, touch, and smell. 'Noticing' is your superpower.

One year, I was at a new school, hired as a kindergarten teacher. During the first week of school it was very difficult for some children to adjust to the new environment and just as difficult for moms and dads to walk out of the classroom. The principal and I encouraged parents to be with their children in the morning, mostly to soothe themselves. After one week, parents were asked to drop the children off and leave before the bell rang. In this particular school, it was the tradition to line the children up at the entrance doors to the school. Then when the bell rang, each class took their turn to enter the building through their own door. My kindergarteners were crying as they waited to enter the building; some out of genuine sadness and the others out of empathy for their new classmates. I was a little slow in catching the outside door before it closed behind the first grade line. I stuck my key in the lock. It was a new copy, but it wouldn't work. We were the only class out there, and all 20 of my kindergarteners were crying. So, providing what the moment called for, I turned and banged on the metal door and shouted, "Little pig! Little pig! Let me in!" I turned and all the children were laughing. That is the power of being present, without your phone in your hand.

The extra rock that you placed on the shelf is to be shared with one other dad; a friend or a relative. When you hand him the rock, you will tell him what you noticed while playing the game. You will tell him how you played the game. The best part is you will pass on the secret code question and secret code answer so that you and he can identify other dads who play the Daddy Rocks game; sort of like secret agents.

Question: Do you rock?
Answer: This daddy rocks!

That way you can identify other dads who are playing the Daddy Rocks game in the gym, at the playground, at community gatherings, and at work. You create your own subculture of dads who help each other with what you noticed and how you responded so that 1) dads don't have to ask for help, and 2) dads remain out from under the purview of the state that wants only to make money off of dads by providing them with conflicting messages, and trying to make dads feel bad. Your best interest is not what they have in mind. Moms have zero access to the game—only dads.

Mindfulness is an experience, not a behavior—that's it, in a nutshell.. Although yoga poses, intentional walking, and meditation may, by chance, provide you with an experience of mindfulness, the behavior is not a prerequisite for experiencing mindfulness. All you do is notice what you see, hear, taste, touch, and smell for a moment. That's the experience of mindfulness. You do that ten times a day, and your life will change.

Never go into the mind without the body. Mindfulness is in the body, not the mind. Mindfulness is an experience, not a behavior. You can experience mindfulness with a rock.

It's that simple.

Dr. Michaela Turner is on a mission to bring mindfulness to life in everyday ordinary moments. With fun and games as the catalyst to create a nano-second of awareness, everyday routines become fun and friendly. The first game was the hide-and-seek Daddy Rocks mindful fathering game from her dissertation (2020).

Dr. Turner is showcasing the 11 other games in her upcoming book. Check out her YouTube

@thejogayogafiles.

Daddy
Daddy

SURVIVING TO THRIVE... WILLIE J.

My heart was nearly torn to shreds at the thought of me not getting to live out the fulfillment of my childhood dreams. I just had to find a way to see the bright light of God within, because the darkness had almost consumed me.

Boy, talk about close calls.

I really do believe in miracles and sometimes they tend to show up as gifts wrapped up in a total disguise. With a new birth of blessings born right from the wombs of our most painful and frustrating moments in life. I'm sure that you can relate to this.

It was about a month before dropping my classic, co-authored book *Rattle Awake: Volume One.* I had already been scheduled simultaneously for two major front cover shoots with Stardom and Morocco Forbes magazine.

They were all geared up now to do an exclusive interview, story and write up about my journey to the top, and the timing and alignment couldn't have been any better.

The editor of Morocco Forbes had just given me the proof. In less than twenty-four hours, I got the most tragic news: the country of Morocco was suddenly hit by a deadly earthquake that killed thousands of innocent people, including little children.

Rest in Peace

I mean, I just couldn't believe what I was even reading or

hearing at that moment. It was all over the news media, social media and my heart became so overwhelmed with the deepest empathy and compassion. Which is why me and my company decided to dedicate one of my newest hit singles entitled "Never Let U Go," to help out with the overall cause.

NOW LET'S TAKE IT BACK A LITTLE BIT IF YOU DONT MIND:

When I gaze back into the lenses of about 3 years ago. I am instantly reminded of a popular quote made by the legendary Maya Angelou who said, "My mission in life is not merely to survive, but thrive; and to do so with some passion, some compassion, some humor, and some style"

I soon discovered that it would not be good enough for me and my company to just survive, but rather thrive, and to level up with more success, more wisdom, more growth, more understanding, more hope, and most of all more love.

Well, this may sound a little odd to you, but that brutal pandemic was when I actually learned my greatest lessons overall. It became my rare golden opportunity to survive, expand and thrive forward against all of the odds against me. This was also the same moment that my company hit the #1 spot in the NY Weekly Top 10 Fastest Growing Companies in 2021.

My whole life has always been about changing and switching my survival mode into my thrive mode. Then I would ask the great God above us all to expose the many hidden gems wrapped up inside of my worst storms. It is the real reason why my hardest lessons in life became my greatest blessings in return.

Yea sure, the investment was a big pain at times, but at the end of it all, the return was also a great gain.

Have you ever felt like giving up on barely making it? Or just merely getting by enough to make ends meet again and again? Or grown tired of going through the same repetitive cycles just to end up nowhere fast? Or would rather be flipping and turning what you have gone through into your greatest achievements, greatest accomplishments, greatest stories, and greatest rewards?

Well, I'm sure that you have - we all have felt those ways at some point in life.

MY MINI FLASHBACKS:

I just couldn't allow all of my pain to be in vain and not gain from it. There just had to be something greater on the horizon or some sort of bright light at the end of these dark tunnels. This became my brand-new mindset after facing prison time, getting cut-up multiple times with a razor blade, losing my cousin Tony to gun violence, and nearly dying on the highway from being sandwiched in between a high-speed chase.

Oh boy, what a narrow escape; I thought that only cats had nine lives, or so they say. lol

No seriously, I had to eventually learn how to maximize my darkest moments and gain some new momentum growing forward.

I like to call it my moments and momentum: take the "um" off of the word momentum and you get the word moment. Our momentum is determined by how well we can maximize or utilize our current moments. It is something that we all must take full advantage of and it is the key ingredient to escaping the common survival mode once and for all.

ME AND MY DAUGHTERS CLOSE CALL:

I can recall a few years back when me and my daughter Jazmine had been traveling home one day. It was just weeks before my forthcoming national front cover shoot. It also became her very first professional magazine print feature, and we were both extremely excited about it beyond description.

When suddenly a man in an unknown vehicle came speeding around the corner erratically, and crashed head-on into a vehicle that was parked on someone else's front lawn. I mean he was barely 20 yards away from us; he could've killed us both in the blink of an eye.

Well, let's just say that I am very, very grateful to God that we are both still alive and breathing well today.

It was absolute pandemonium. People were racing from everywhere, screaming loudly with deep panic inside of their voices

So, me and my daughter decided to get out of the car and check on him momentarily, only to find him lying there lifeless next to his own damaged truck, drowning in a pool of his own blood.

I'm talking about a real life, full-blown nightmare here that had shown up on both of our streets completely unannounced. However, with the help of God we were both able to fully recover and heal expeditiously.

Fortunately, we were able to thrive all of the way to the

photo shoot. It ended up being a big hit and a huge success overall.

WHEN CYBER BULLYING GOES WRONG:

Shortly after releasing my hit records "In the Morning" and "We Love You Puerto Rico," featuring various artists, I was asked to write another charity-based hit record. But this time it would be for a beautiful young teenager named Isabel, who had been bullied constantly at her school by way of social media. How sad that it resulted in her taking her life at a very young and tender age.

Man, was I not completely blown-away and deeply moved by this most tragic story as told by her mom and my business partner Aaron Emig, especially since it occurred so close to our hometown. She was also one of the actual victims who had suffered from the Hurricane Maria catastrophe.

The good news is that we all put on a very successful outdoor concert event in memory of her, including some great donations and proceeds given towards the actual cause that day.

Our sole purpose for this event was to help prevent more teens from committing suicide under very intense social pressure. Shortly afterwards, we heard the great news that an 11-year-old kid who had attended the event got empowered and decided to live on; to keep his life moving forward.

"Now that's what I'm talking about, baby." We continue to SURVIVE and THRIVE by showing others how to do the same.

That is the real reason why we sing, the real reason why we

write, the real reason why we coach, the real reason why we speak, the real reason why we lead, and the real reason why we succeed in the first place.

We absolutely strive to create everlasting hope for all generations to come.

Afterall, we are all in this thing together and together we can do the impossible. We can all look forward to a brighter future, a brighter day, and a better tomorrow. Because each breath taken is a new moment, and each new moment is a new opportunity to grow further into our new future.

We must keep the big vision alive and realize that true greatness comes along with a healthy price, and with some great struggle. The late great Freddrick Douglas said,

"Without struggle there could be no progress."

So let us never lose hope in ourselves, hope in others, hope in our dreams, hope in our goals, hope in love, and hope in our God-Given potential to be great in life one day.

Willie J is on a mission to empower more people and change more lives while creating more hope through arts, business, coaching and entertainment. As a world-renowned entrepreneur, author, artist, speaker and coach of the John Maxwell Team, this St. Louis native has been featured as a Top Entrepreneur in both Forbes and GQ Magazine. His company, Pure Mission Entertainment, hit #1 in the top 10 spots of NY Weekly, LA Weekly, LA Wire, and US Reporter, to name just a few outstanding accolades. Most recently he graced the front cover of the "Los Angeles Magazine" with an article that can be read on his company website: puremissionent.com

MIRACLES ON THE PLAYGROUND...
CHIYEDZA NYAHUYE

Every man gotta right to decide his own destiny...

~ Bob Marley, Zimbabwe

I had to find a way to reinvent myself because working in minimum wage jobs with a Master's degree was making me feel like such a failure. The kool-aid formula of going to school, getting good grades, and then landing a good-paying job with benefits did not work for me. Rather ironic since I had finished high school in Hong Kong, China, and got 2 degrees in the Twin Cities of Minnesota, USA, all on full-ride scholarships.

I went back to Zimbabwe and spent 14 years trying to actualize the "education promise" but to no avail. Over 700 applications and never got a job that way. Whichever consultancies I got were by word-of-mouth referrals from friends and expat colleagues. Yet, there was another underlying running theme coloring this situation. Though I had been successful in academic excellence, (which was body armor that I built to protect myself from unsafe, vulnerable home situations as a child), I couldn't seem to align with the UN gravy train of more lucrative high-paying roles that I was more than qualified for. I seemed to fall into the trap of working so hard, multiplying the revenues and funding of other people's companies and NGOs, yet getting paid so little to do so. After several years of doing that, it became a self-fulfilling prophecy that I was not worthy of receiving the high income to build a decent life or lifestyle, let alone thrive.

Things dried up for me in early 2018, when I got fired for missing a day of work -it was my birthday and we had agreed on the day off a month before. You have to wonder, after being mad, then sad, if these 'events' are "good." I was helping diasporan Zimbabweans build their dream houses in the country. I had agreed to be paid $300 per month, working 14+ hours daily across global time zones, as Head of Projects. I was also in a vulnerable position due to political situations that were getting more precarious due to my affiliations.

Then knowing how God works, when it's enough, it's enough. My younger sister is best friends with a cousin I had never met. He was living with his family in the USA. She continued to insist I contact him. She felt strongly that he could help me move back there. I was afraid of being a burden, not wanting to rely on a man and his wife to support and take care of me. He, a pastor and biochemist, and his wife, a hydrology engineer, already had 6 children in the home, with Grandpa too. Choosing to take on my process of relocation, through the asylum process, was definitely quite an undertaking. I finally agreed to come and within 3 weeks of saying yes, I was in the Harare airport. After tearful goodbyes to my mother, sisters, and niece, I flew out.

I had been sold on the idea that I would only be with my cousin and his family for four months whilst getting my papers ready to be able to work, then I could find my own place. Turned out to be a full year. I am grateful for President Trump's policy at the time of last in, first processed in terms of asylum status interviews. Within six weeks of applying for asylum, I was granted an interview in Chicago. I didn't realize that it would then be another six months before I could get my work permit and social security allocation.

In the meantime, living with my beloved cousin and his family had its challenges. I found myself making myself smaller and almost invisible because I felt terribly guilty for the sacrifices they were making for me being in their home. I did what I could to help around the house. Their three little boys, aged 2, 4 and 6 at the time, would be screaming and fighting for hours, every single day. It was rather trying since I was cooped up and could hardly leave the house. They would shout at me," Shut up auntie, you're stupid, I'll kill you!" At first, I was offended, then of course I understood children pushing buttons in their frustration to communicate. So, I would respond, "Oh you want to kill me? Come here and I'll show you how to kill me nicely." And so, when they came over, I would wrap my arms around them, tickle them silly, and have them squealing in delirious delight! In transforming that energy, they would often come peep round the door, with mischievous twinkles in their eyes, saying, "Auntie, can I kill you?" and all I had to do was raise my hands like claws and they would burst into giggles running up the stairs, yelling, "No Auntie, no tickles!" and I didn't even touch them!

It's amazing how a 7am-4pm "long walk" on Saturdays helped with a much-needed break for us all. You would have found me sitting at the park with chocolate-covered fingers and a smile. But that was only until November. It was getting colder, and I couldn't go out. So yes mentally and emotionally it did get rather intense for me. Don't get me wrong, I am forever grateful to my cousin and his wife for their generosity and kindness, but we are human after all.

I hustled to earn money and move. Two minimum wage jobs took a toll, but I knew my being there for so long did, too. It was time for me to move out; disappear for a while. So even during Covid, having tried some entrepreneurial ventures and been duped twice, I received an eviction notice. I didn't say anything to my cousin. Thank goodness there was also a government directive to not evict people due to the public health crisis. I was able to submit the required stay-in-place form to the apartment complex office.

I continued to struggle to figure out how to make more than the minimum wage earnings. I switched to two other jobs that were located in a shopping center behind my apartment complex. Since I didn't have a car, it made economic sense. I was still baffled by how I continued to live such a limited life with all my educational background and experiences. I felt that I couldn't apply for jobs in offices as the costs of getting to and from those jobs would be astronomical and the bus system access was over a mile away. Trudging a mile through snow didn't make sense to me.

Yet, when it was time to move on, just like when I was plucked out of Zimbabwe, the 2021 Covid vaccination drives were my way out. A co-worker connected me to a staffing agency. I was first told that we needed to speak Spanish fluently to be assigned to California, and were put on a waiting list for other options. However, one fateful

Tuesday on my day off, as I was about to do my grocery shopping, I received a call from the staffing agency. They wanted to know if I could be ready to get on a plane the next day for Los Angeles. They needed two people, so I put in my co-worker's name. We had plane tickets processed before we even signed the actual contracts two hours later. We quickly went shopping for scrubs for the role, and the next day, quit our jobs and flew out to LA.

The main lesson of receiving during this experience was working less and being paid more. We were housed at the Courtyard Marriott in Rancho Cucamonga, bussed to and from work in Pomona, and given two meals a day. You could figure out how to work seven days a week if you wanted to. We really only worked for 5 ½ hours or so per day but got paid for ten. This was the most money I had made at 40+ years old. I managed to pay off debts, and sent money to my mother in Zimbabwe, who then bought herself a brand new Defy fridge. I quickly got promoted to team lead in coordinating the timely vaccine distribution to the nurses administering them, with a team of five daily. I also explored LA beaches, national parks, and even went horse riding in the Hollywood hills on my weekly day off. Yet the contract got shortened and I was back in Ohio four months later. Tried a stint selling health and life insurance and after over 90 hours of work, only made $369 in commissions. Like they say here in the US, "If the coin ain't right, say goodnight!" Well, my goodnight came in the form of a YouTube ad for SV Academy. I was literally on my knees after a Thursday of 14 canceled back-to-back appointments and wondering, surely there is no way that this would become the rest of my life.

So, when SV Academy found me in August 2021, not only

did I successfully complete the program but was invited to join the team. As a Program Manager, it wasn't enough for me to just put the learners through the paces of the intensely rigorous 4 or 8-week training programs, but to also fast-track getting them hired in tech sales and fulfill the promised mandate.

I was privileged to work with mainly black and brown career transitioning, brilliant and multi-talented professionals. I found myself being a catalyst of zones of genius and a translator of professional skills and capabilities into SDR (Sales Development Representative) verbiage, whilst keeping it fun. Being a part-time evening cohort trainer, I empathized with these already inundated learners. They would arrive on Zoom, exhausted from juggling demanding days and responsibilities. I started classes with energizing music, in-chair gentle yoga stretches, and breathing centering exercises. I kept it engaging and entertaining with humor, my British references, and questioning certain American expressions. I also found ways to connect with each individual learner to ensure a productive experience. I even described the relationship between Coursera SV Academy modules as their encyclopedia of knowledge, and me being the TikTok version. After evening classes, having stopped recording the lesson, we would have our "shoot the breeze" time even having music jam sessions and serenades of original songs! There seemed to be several artists and musicians in my classes. Work can be creative and playful too, and that's where genius and performance metrics thrive!

I intentionally promoted and developed research-based multi-channel, multimedia, multi-touch campaigns for the interview processes, including creative video touches in LinkedIn connection messages. For those who fully implemented them, there were at least three who got hired the day they graduated from the SV Academy training. A recent grad was asked by her now-current employer to teach her peers how to replicate these tactics in prospecting for new clients.

However, in May of 2023, my season at SV Academy came to an end due to a massive company reduction. In the spirit of #FactsTellStoriesSell, a quote from my network marketing personal development training days, I decided to re-introduce myself to the Saas, Tech industry through personal anecdotal posts on LinkedIn. I saw this as a way to bring the resume bullets to life, demonstrating to the sales professional empathetic emotional intelligence and the people-centered capacity-building skills I have; truly, undeniable assets.

I enthusiastically engaged in LinkedIn live sessions and audio rooms. I actively gave emoji reactions to points that resonated with me whilst the hosts and guests were sharing their gems of expertise. I would also follow up with detailed connecting messages to those who spoke as I felt moved. I devised a system where I would create the connection message while they were speaking. I had to be economical with my attention span, especially when you have a panel of 4-7 professional development experts, including the host, and wanting to grab a nugget from each one! So, I would listen to each speaker on the LinkedIn live on my phone, and grab onto one nugget that I immediately included in my direct message to them from my laptop. When speakers offered for listeners to reach out to them and schedule free virtual coffees to connect, being a good student, I took them all up on it. That's where the miracles started to unfold on this playground.

I met with a recruiter, Joi the Joiful Recruiter, who is so compassionate and brilliantly talented in all she does. I felt like I gained a sister instantly. She recommended me to more recruiters and influential, successful black women. Within 20 minutes of our first phone conversation, I was invited to be a guest with the phenomenal sales guru, Cherilynn Castleman, on her LinkedIn live session, "Empowering Women to Soar in the World of Sales." She loved how I created sixty-second videos on Loom to introduce myself and confirm appointments. Tapping into my network and community engagement tactics, we had women and men tuning in from countries on five continents.

Due to my connector nature, and referring my network to various entrepreneurs for specific expertise, I also gained a masterful, expert sales coach. More virtual coffees hooked me up with job interviews and expanded my professional networks in the tech industry.

The LinkedIn audio rooms took the miracles to a whole 'nother level. I attended sessions on the power of storytelling in rebranding, hosted by the gracious godmother of audio rooms, Angelica Corral. She introduced me to the main hub, co-hosted by the godfather of audio rooms, UK-based Eny Osung. I didn't speak in any of these rooms for the first two months. I would listen, and respond to shares with emojis, but waited until it felt right to raise my hand to get on stage. I chose instead to DM speakers and hosts, thanking them for what they shared or what touched me. All my comments were warmly received. Then one day I heard it was Eny's birthday, so I sang him my own cultural version of Happy Birthday using the Loom app for recording. Though I sent it to him as a DM, next thing I knew, it was going viral on LinkedIn! I still have prominent audio room hosts referring to that gesture of just admiring me being my true uncensored self. Eny also has this very Papa, diplomatic-type vibe. He intentionally welcomes people in the rooms individually by name, highlighting their expertise. His tagline is that he makes people famous. Before I knew it, he was introducing me as a global sales leader, a sales guru! This was before we even had our first 1:1. In the first three and a half months, I only raised my hand to be brought on the audio room stage five or six times. On two of those occasions, all I offered was a cultural song that intuitively made sense for the contextual emotions of the conversation.

These audio rooms resulted in invitations to contribute chapters to two international best-selling anthologies. My LinkedIn followers skyrocketed by over a thousand in just two and a half months! The wealth of genuine, kind, loving friendships continues to blossom in these global LinkedIn audio room communities of entrepreneurs.

I landed two jobs by mid-August; both through my SV Academy networks. Rahim Fazal, the CEO of SV Academy, recommended me to the hiring manager at MineralTree who is an SV grad, and then my ex-coworker and dear friend Myn got me hired into a part-time role with Coursera. I continue to emphasize it's not so much about who you know, but who knows you and how they know you.

I am grateful for how quickly I received both of these opportunities within a three-month period of job hunting. However, I started having rapid heart palpitations that would wake me up in the middle of the night. I wasn't sleeping until maybe 4 a.m. I found myself weeping uncontrollably, feeling drained and exhausted all the time. I hardly let anyone see that side of me, and only more recently shared about it as an after-fact with a few family members.

So, my breakdown happened in an intentional virtual healing circle of professional African diaspora women that we co-created three years ago. This was the week before I did my LinkedIn live event with Cherilynn. I had been having a rough day after so many rejection emails, and my finances were strained. I had paid my August rent but literally had $100 left. So when we met that fateful Tuesday, Dr. Semerit welcomed us to breathe deeply, feel into our bodies, and say one word that arose. I felt so vulnerable. She invited me to pause my giggly bubbliness and allow my full self to just be. I watched my sisters share their moving stories and when it was my turn, I just broke down crying, you know, that ugly cry, where fluids pour out your eyes, nose, and mouth? Yup, that was me. I was rather shocked at myself as I have never, even in the years of our circle, shown that part of me. Dr. Semerit invited my sisters to just be present with me, and resist acting on the instinct to dispel my discomfort. I wailed so deeply, it felt so raw, like my heart was tearing open. I am so used to being the one holding space for people to process their emotions. I have 14 nieces and nephews, and I don't think any of them have ever seen me cry that way. Yet it needed to happen. The love and support I felt in that Zoom room from all these beautiful soul mothers and sisters witnessing my breaking open and rebirthing still makes me weep with deep appreciation.

I scheduled follow-up sessions with Dr. Semerit that week.

Something magical started happening every time we met. So the next day after my heart broke open, and just as I was meeting with Dr. Semerit, my phone kept pinging. I checked later and saw I was being invited by a recruiter to meet with Jake, the hiring manager from MineralTree for an interview the next day. Then that Friday, I was about to have another session with Dr. Semerit, and my friend Myn called me just before letting me know about the Coursera gig and asked me if I wanted it. Of course! The recruiter was also calling me during my session that afternoon. I called her back and secured the Coursera job, too. I started thinking that hmmm, Dr. Semerit must be my juju, my good luck charm, jobs manifesting each time I was deepening my inner healing work; outwardly, it quickly yielded powerful results. Two of my soul sisters sent me a gorgeous bouquet of flowers with tiger lilies that same Thursday. The following week, I received an unexpected check from a previous job in the mail and an outstanding direct deposit from another in my bank account. I had allowed myself to borrow some money from a friend to tide me over for groceries and personal items etc, but when the deposits came through, I quickly reimbursed her.

Cherilynn is still my wonderful career coach. She has been instrumental in encouraging me to stay focused on the bigger picture. Yes, I am grateful for the two jobs that are replenishing my finances, but Cherilynn is still having me stay laser-focused on the C-Suite ambitions that I am growing into. I continue visualizing myself as a Global Leader in Strategic Partnerships in Enterprise Sales for a start, but God only knows.

In the meantime, I continue embracing more opportunities arising through my LinkedIn audio rooms community, which are leading me into writing and speaking engagements. Watching the mysteries of my heartbreak, anxieties that kept me up at night that are still fading, my renewed energy thanks to sleeping through the night, and waking up feeling more energized, ready for the day. I am grateful for this season of job hunting and never-ending growth, healing my abilities to receive, bringing to life my own #ChiyedzaEffect, and attracting so many new, soul-enriching relationships and interactions, with more adventures to come.

Exponential growth and strong relationships came as a direct result of those audio- and LinkedIn live events. It costs nothing to attend, to make yourself visible by taking the stage, or simply using emoji reactions to those speaking on stage. I have since learned I don't need two devices in order to message a speaker or audience member: just click their picture and LinkedIn will take you to their profile page without closing the audio room. Check out Loom app for recording, too. It is an easy way of connecting with others and showing your personality. After all, miracles on the playground happen when others get to know the real you. So go ahead and show them how they impacted your day - they will remember you for it.

Chiyedza Nyahuye is on a mission to co-create healthy, vibrant, and engaging environments to enable people to discover and develop their zones of genius. Chiyedza continues to expand her global sales career while building her networks through LinkedIn audio rooms. She is embarking on becoming a keynote speaker to share her multifaceted gifts and expertise, being that light that melts away the darkness. You
can find her on LinkedIn at: **https://www.linkedin.com/**

in/chiyedza-nyahuye-a3770716/

YOU ARE THE LIGHT IN THE BASEMENT... BRIAN SCHULMAN

"Check on the light bulbs before they go out" - *Rachel Druckenmiller*

Have you had a rattled awake moment that you had to get away from? A moment that made you better, not bitter, but maybe not at first? I'm still finding the joy in mine, in spite of all the disappointments. We've all been through that. Radiating Real - I haven't been real for some time.

Maybe you were lucky like me and had a friend who reminded me of the importance of being real. Or maybe you had to do it all on your own.

I sit here writing this, and, if I'm really radiating real, I am terrified to share it...but, I am doing so because I know that there are others who have been going through a similar experience: suffering in silence. I want you to know that you are not alone, and I want to help lift you out of the dark place you are in.

Inside of you, you have a more powerful story than you can imagine; one that will change another's life just by having been you - and what a privilege.

It's easy to put up a facade. It's so much harder to radiate real, and put yourself on a ledge.

I felt like everything was crumbling around me. Like a building had fallen on top of me and knocked all the air out of my lungs. I couldn't breathe. I was alone. Alone on an island that was so quiet you could hear a whisper from the other side. Struggling in silence. Look at what it's taken me to get here. Do I deserve happiness?

I am going through a divorce. There, I said it. Uncharted territory on so many levels. I have always been a "Family First" man. I married a woman I loved deeply. We have 2 beautiful, smart, funny, kind, achieving children together. I worked hard making sure they all had everything they needed and wanted. I wrote my wife poems and gave her flowers for no reason. I made sure my kids could see and feel the love I had for her. When my kids were growing up, I never missed a single practice, performance, or event.

Divorce was not an option in my book, until I realized, for all the ways I was modeling being a good father, partner and family man, one lesson I was teaching my kids was outshining all the others. Not unlike other marriages, over the years my wife and I spent less and less time together. We were busy with the kids. Busy with work. Tired from all the above. At least, that is what I told myself. We weren't connecting…connected. Neither of us did anything 'wrong' by social standards. There was nobody and nothing to blame. We changed over time and that impacted our relationship. The example of what it is to… 'love and be loved unconditionally', 'live in joy' and the ways families care for one another had also changed.

Starting, and going through, the divorce process has been, and remains, the hardest thing I have ever had to face in my life. It has also been my biggest place of growth. On my birthday this year, I celebrated. Me. My children. The growth I have fought hard for. At 48 years old, I chose JOY.

You see, my promise, as a father, as a husband, as a human,

is that I would teach my kids something I realized I was not 'taught:' that they deserve to be loved unconditionally and what the person you love deserves in return - but I was no longer doing that.

I realized I was robbing my kids of a healthy model of love that would impact them the rest of their lives. I knew, no matter how hard and painful it would be, I owed it to them to fulfill that promise.

When I shared about my divorce on LinkedIn, #RadiatingReal, I got SUPER vulnerable. While I have shared about growing up a one-and-a-half pound (yes, you read that right) miracle baby in the 70's that wasn't supposed to live, twitching and ticking my way through life with a neurological disorder, Tourette's Syndrome, being bullied, teased and outcasted and failing more than I succeeded in life and in business - this was different. That was all in the PAST. THIS is now. It is real and raw. And sharing it made me feel as if I were naked in front of a crowd. But people showed up for me in such beautiful ways. And in sharing MY story, I was showing up for others, giving permission to share their stories.

I sat in front of my computer terrified to hit 'post' on LinkedIn. Four pictures were staring back at me from the screen, sharing tears of pain, fear, sadness, frustrations, anguish, flowing so others would know that they are not alone - and to remind myself that I am not alone.

For the past year I have been surviving. I have been exhausted down to my bones. I have been fighting myself every day to 'get things done,' I have not felt like myself. I have not felt confident. I have felt heavy – weighed down. I have felt my light dimming. I have been terrified of feeling what I have been feeling, because it feels like I will shatter to pieces. It feels like if the flood gates would open I would drown, but by locking 'those' feelings away, I have also locked away joy, happiness, contentment.

You know that feeling? That 'lack of' feeling?

I convinced myself it was better and I had it under control. In reality, for the last year, those emotions have had total control over my entire life and every decision I've made, until I let the floodgates open. It did not magically make everything better, but it did get better.

Divorce has been the hardest thing I have ever had to do in my life, and the hardest decision I have ever had to make. And I am so grateful.

No matter how many times I have been hit, have fallen, felt like I was in the dark alone in the basement, reality is, we are never alone, and WE ARE the light in the basement - we just can't see it.

I have and continue to fight with my inner bully, struggling, grieving, constantly asking - DO I deserve happiness? Truth is, we all do.

It doesn't need to end with a neat and tidy bow. It's a process and life. I was rattled awake by a journey I didn't even know I was on and it has been, as a friend of mine says, *ugly, snotty and unsexy*, but I have been able to recognize pivots of joy. And that is progress.

What I've realized is that for a long time I have carried the weight of past mistakes. I have allowed past mistakes to define my self-worth, to shape my self-perception, and honestly, I have been my own harshest critic. I think it's something many of us can relate to.

Replaying moments of perceived failure over and over in my mind. 23 years of marriage. A year of divorce. A year of pain. A year of uncertainties. A year of disruptions. A year... of growth.

Recently a good friend and I got on a video chat together, and he said something that hit me hard.

"I don't think you've forgiven yourself," he said.

It shook me to my core. What did he just say? Everything around me went silent, as my eyes filled with tears and I heard it again in my head. I hadn't forgiven myself.

What I have come to learn is that forgiveness begins within and it's a conscious choice, to release the burdens of guilt and self-blame; understanding that I deserve the same kindness and understanding that I readily offer to others. Understanding that self-forgiveness isn't about absolving responsibility or ignoring the consequences of our actions; it's about acknowledging the past. It's learning from the past. And it's letting go of the past.

It's about reclaiming our own power, freeing ourselves from the shackles of regret, and realizing that this whole journey we are on, has and continues to be a really powerful reminder; that growth often arises from the ashes of these "mistakes." Mistakes that are moments. Moments of vulnerability, where we find our strength. Moments of vulnerability, where we evolve. Moments of vulnerability, where we adapt. And moments of vulnerability, where we become more resilient.

We are all a work in progress. And now more than ever, our

greatest lessons often emerge from our most challenging moments. We all make mistakes. It's an inevitable part of being human.

The past year has been a rollercoaster for me, marked by pain, uncertainties, disruptions and growth. I have faced the heart-wrenching reality of being physically apart from my kids. A year of calls, text messages and counting down the days until we could be together again. After not seeing my son for a year, getting to finally see him face-to-face again, the emotions overwhelmed me. Tears of joy, laughter, and an overwhelming sense of gratitude for this incredible young man. No words could capture what my heart felt. It was a gift, this precious time with my son.

My son has grown so much in the past year, his resilience, strength, and unwavering optimism in the face of adversity, inspire me every day. It's a reminder that even in the toughest times we have the power to grow and emerge stronger. It's a testament to the power of love, patience and the unwavering bonds that connect us as families. It's a reminder to all of us that no matter the distance, or the circumstances, love knows no boundaries.

It's been 20 months (608.74 days) since I've spoken to my daughter. I know that the time with her will come, too, and how incredibly grateful I am for that moment.

As parents, we constantly strive to provide our children with the best opportunities to be there for them, cheer them on, love them unconditionally with all our heart, to listen, and to witness their growth firsthand.

When circumstances challenge us to be apart, we learn the true value of connection and cherishing every moment together.

I want to take a moment to express my love, appreciation and gratitude for the incredible support of my colleagues, friends, my LinkedInFam, an incredible heart-filled community, and complete strangers. Your encouragement and positivity have been a source of strength throughout my journey of divorce these last 15 months.

In sharing these moments with my LinkedInFam and you, the reader, I hope to inspire others who may be separated from their loved ones, to remind you that even when your world, when the world, feels uncertain, the love that unites us remains steadfast.

I have experienced a year filled with challenges, a year of separation, and a year filled with more growth than I can fully comprehend. However, I know it's there.

You've been reading this, and have bravely shared with yourself that you're battling uphill. Stuck in the wet cement. Feel like you can't breathe. Too stressed to smile, juggling challenges left and right. Wondering if you'll ever catch a break. I've been there too. I AM there.

But let me tell you, amidst the struggles, there is untapped potential waiting to be unleashed within each of us. Like a seed pushing through the darkness to reach the sunlight, we, too, must persevere. It's during these trying times that we grow, learn, and evolve. Together.

We must embrace the struggle, for it is the catalyst for greatness. The magic lies in recognizing that we can thrive even in the face of adversity. It's not about waiting for perfect circumstances but making the best out of what we have, right now. It's about finding opportunities in every obstacle and turning challenges into stepping stones.

So, how can we keep going? How can we transform struggle into growth and prosperity?

We can embrace resilience and develop a mindset that views setbacks as stepping stones, not roadblocks; and remember that resilience is the key to turning challenges into opportunities.

We can embrace our imperfections and understand that perfection is an illusion; choose to focus on progress, rather than absolute flawlessness. Be FLAWSOME. Be perfectly, imperfectly you!

We can embrace self-compassion and be kind to ourselves during tough times, treating ourselves with the same love and support we'd offer a dear friend.

We can embrace adaptability, change and be willing to adapt our strategies as needed. The ability to pivot and stay agile is vital in a world full of so many uncertainties.

We can embrace gratitude and count our blessings, no matter how small, as gratitude shifts our perspective and helps us see the silver lining in challenging situations.

When we encourage each other to keep moving forward, even when the path seems unclear, we feel like maybe, we truly can keep moving forward.

I have come to understand that the most crucial journey we can embark upon is the journey of self-compassion; it's about recognizing that I, like everyone else, am a work in progress. It's about accepting that making 'mistakes,' which aren't in fact mistakes, doesn't diminish your value, it's simply a stepping stone on the path of growing.

Not unlike a rubber-band stretched beyond its capacity, life sometimes feels like it's going to snap right between our fingers. What I've come to understand is that, like a rubber-band on a slingshot, it's pulling us back further and further, not to hold us back, but to gain power and exponentially propel us FORWARD. So, when you doubt yourself, take a deep breath in, smile and offer gratitude for the moment. Know that what lies ahead will be better than you imagined and, ALWAYS, put good out into the universe to help others, no matter what you are going through. Breathe, and remind yourself, the next great chapter of the adventure in the journey is unfolding right before you, and you are exactly where you are meant to be.

Remember, within every struggle lies an opportunity to thrive, and together, we have created a supportive community that fosters growth, resilience and success.

In my darkest days of desperation, my community, my LinkedInFam, gave me hope.

Let's embrace the journey, knowing that we are capable of thriving amidst the struggles, together.

Let's keep pushing ourselves to new heights and celebrating each victory in our journey, learning from every setback, together.

Life's journey is a rollercoaster ride where struggles and triumphs dance together in perfect harmony, and together, there is nothing we cannot get through.

As we move forward, let's continue to love, to appreciate and nurture the precious bonds that tie. Let's continue to cherish the moments together; the moments with your loved ones. For they, YOU, are the true treasures in life.

So, here's to intention. Here's to self-forgiveness. Here's to self-compassion. Here's to the unshakeable belief, that we have the power to rewrite our own narratives. And here's to all of us being a part of each other's journey.

Brian Schulman is on a mission to change the landscape of how we do business through Voice Your Vibe's groundbreaking masterminds and his heart-centered leadership programs. Named 'The King Of Community on LinkedIn' by Forbes and known as the Godfather, and Pioneer, of LinkedIn Video and one of the world premiere live streaming & video marketing experts, Brian Schulman is a 10X #1 Best-Selling Author and internationally known Keynote Speaker recognized by LinkedIn as a 3X Top Voice in Leadership & Digital Strategy, 3X Top 50 Most Impactful People of LinkedIn, 4X Rising Star & Influencer To Watch on LinkedIn and 2X LinkedIn Global Leader of the year out of ~1 Billion business professionals, whose expertise, insights & 2 Global Award-Winning LinkedIn LIVE Shows co-hosted with Nancy Debra Barrows, have been featured on NASDAQ, Forbes, Thrive Global, Yahoo Finance, Bloomberg, Viacom, Roku TV, Amazon Fire, PODTV, The CW, multiple #1 best-selling books, syndicated on Smart TV Networks & hundreds of shows & podcasts, reaching millions world-wide.Â Connect with him here:

https://www.voiceyourvibe.com

MASTERING MYSTICISM AND PREVAILING!... NIKI BELL

The blackness of the night enveloped my senses. The darkness penetrated my third eye and I could not see what was coming for me. My crown chakra, destroyed. I only could feel something was deathly wrong. The mysteries of the sea kept coming with the waves rolling into one all-consuming overtaking of my consciousness. I proclaimed from within: I am a GODDESS! I am LOVE! I am the SUN! The universe is within me. I am the universe! Goddess- is the divine spirit within and many spiritualities, religions, and myths believe in this. I am Buddha! An enlightened being with wisdom. I am everything to me because I have always believed in myself, no matter what was presented to me at the time. I have always been keenly aware of my rights.

Most times, I am a physical being having a spiritual experience and an awakening to the causality of latent effects. My power comes from within which is void of any attachments, physical or spiritual. Light and dark is within us and we attract situations and people accordingly. It is knowing my rights, spiritually and physically, that has set me free time and time again.

The only person that can validate me, my story, my worth, my self, my soul, my being… is me. I am alone in all that I do and I have always been alone. It is by the sure power of the spiritual and physical; a universe testing me every step of the way. I only wish it would stop. In this story, by knowing my rights - both physically and spiritually - you see how I stopped myself from drowning in the proverbial swelling of the seas as the ground floor was swept out from under me.

I have gone through so much beauty in life that the ugliness of it stands out so obviously and instantly. I take responsibility for my life, without self-blame, for absolutely being oblivious to evil and demonic persons that hide behind silk words and silk clothing. I just didn't see it coming. This is why I am compelled to share with you how I managed to escape more than one of these evil people in a single night. It is because I know my rights.

On a nice cool night, I can feel the Delta breeze on my face. I can smell the unfortunate city air where our homeless lie in the wake. I hear the screams of violence rip through my city. I see couples holding hands and others fighting. Yet, I stand still, uninvolved and unwilling to engage; I only wish to inspire. Every day and with every breath I take, I am cosmically aware of my time, place, space, and in this reality. I spiritually align myself by chanting a powerful mantra throughout the day. Still, I cannot fathom why someone would want to do this to me.

I was assaulted in all kinds of ways by a male that I met through online dating less than a week before our fateful date. I was coerced to take edibles, only to discover they were laced. I was coerced to drink a tall glass of vodka and orange juice, known as a screwdriver. This was consumed right after having the gummy worms. It is not weak of a strong woman to go through this, or to be coerced into doing something that she would not normally do. "Coercion" from the Office of Women's Health states, "Sexual coercion is when a person pressures, tricks, threatens, or manipulates someone into having sex. It is a type of sexual assault because even if someone says yes, they are not giving their consent freely."

It is slanderous for me to have self-pity, arrogance, ego, shame, or guilt, for example. In my years of hardships, I have mastered the ability to not do that to myself, no matter what the situation may be. I have been fighting for my right to be treated with human decency rather than like a sex slave my entire life. On this night I was disillusioned, the opposite of enlightenment. If I was to give pause, which I did, one would think it was too late. It was not! I had to save myself and all universal forces had to come to my aid once activated.

I have no history of recreational drugs. I have debilitating health and on occasion I am visibly disabled. I do not have a support system, friends, or family, all due to my need to overcome 30 plus years of sexual trafficking, domestic violence, psychological torture, emotional abuse, verbal retaliation on my ears every day of my life, and financial ramifications as a direct cause and result of all mentioned. These major crises of events have not ever stopped, nor have I ever stopped fighting because I know my rights. My perspective about these crises has changed for the better. I was born into this kind of world, but it does not mean I have to put up with it, live in it, be disempowered by it, or continue to be victimized.

The resistance to the change that one seeks should not be so convoluted that there is no resolve or relief. I know that I attracted what I needed to be changed and that by putting a voice to it, the change has already occurred. I chose to be here on Earth. I chose these experiences. My soul has lived on forever, lifetime after lifetime, and it will continue to do so. The mantra I chant is to eradicate my karma at its core in this lifetime. It is not when I die that my karma will change. It is while I am alive that it will change, in order for me to be happy. I must give myself permission to continue to be a seeking spirit, to teach, and learn from others. Karma is cause and effect. Karma is also Universal law, whether one believes in it or not, it exists in our lives. If you do good then good will come unto you. As an enlightened being, I still have human experiences, my immortal soul rises up to overcome that physical manifested effect. Cause and effect can happen in a single moment, not just in a past life. We are constantly making causes and having an effect on ourselves, on others, and our environment. For there to be growth in this lifetime and the next, my determination - my prayer - is to overcome challenges in order to remain happy from within.

I have WON in all aspects of LIFE! I win through pure LOVE for myself and others! I continue to dance to my soft salsa music, twirling in the wind, smiling and happy. This I do daily while reaching for my Goddess power within, bringing forth a soul that is healed, a mind that is sharp, and a heart that does not stop bleeding. I rely heavily on my gifts and when I venture away from them... I proclaim, "I love you, Niki. You are a gentle soul. A kind, loving, sensual, amazing human being. You are complete and perfect as you are. I love you, Niki." I hug myself because no one ever has. I am confident within myself.

In spite of my resolve to move beyond such dreadful events, to embrace the experience if only to transmute and dissolve its origins, I *continue* to be 'punished' for reasons I cannot fathom. This is the light and darkness that many of us possess. This is the physical being trying to understand the spiritual experience. This is the mortal part of me. Out of the darkness one can see the light and awaken to their mission.

Speaking of darkness, there were quite a bit of red flags with this guy. The last 'event' was at a restaurant. During dinner the drugs were setting in and the alcohol was speeding it along. I saw something in my date that I did not catch before, a sickness around the beaming of his eyes, a quiet anticipation of what is to come, and a deep-seated-hatred for women all along. I sensed a concern in his eyes; worry that I'd found him out. Yes, indeed I had! But I was too drugged and almost too weak to move. And he knew this would happen, my sudden realization. He had to be sure that he would still have his way with me. All I could think was to get out of there and go somewhere safe. THIS IS MY SPIRITUAL RIGHT- TO BE SAFE! I told my date I had to use the restroom and grabbed my purse. I went to the bar of the restaurant to ask for help, informing them that I was not safe with my date. As I swayed back and forth, I stated I wanted to call ride share and go home. A while later, they asked if they should call the police, but that was six minutes before my ride was due to arrive. The call to the police should have been done the moment I said I did not feel safe. In some odd way, I was protected by things not being done properly.

Once in the rideshare, my life was further in jeopardy. I did call 9-1-1 after I was escorted from the bar to the rideshare vehicle. The manager explained to the driver that I had been drugged, needed to call 9-1-1, and get home. The manager should have never told the driver that much information, especially the part of me being drugged.

The next hour was a complete nightmare that I could not come out of. I was dropped from the Red Sea into the black ocean and headed to the ocean floor with every turn on the winding roads. My mind and body kept slipping into its abyss; the more I kicked and tried to come up for air, the more I could not. The mind and my forehead were completely black. I could not look up. My third eye could not see, my abilities were gone, I thought! All except the use of my mind to fight what was happening. My mind, especially in this instance, is my life.

My toddler training on sexual warfare at the forefront of enemy lines came into play when I was then being sexually assaulted. Also, my life as an adult, where I tactfully had to explain things without criminalizing myself, came from my tortured soul and all in one voice. I *had* to make my mind overpower the drugs in order to come up and speak out. I did not have all my faculties intact. I had to make sense of things that did not make sense. I was more attuned to what was going on, more so even, than if I was not drugged. The power of the mind is priceless. The power of my life experiences is one in and of the same. I knew I had the right to ask for help. I had the right to call the police. I had the right to report my date and my driver.

The authorities on the 9-1-1 call would not help after racially profiling me. They laughed at me. I let them know that while being drugged, they were putting my life in further danger. I knew I had the right to speak in such a way because I was not a victim. I was an empowered Warrior Goddess! Fighting! Fighting! Fighting for my life. I asked them if they understood that they were not helpful at all. They simply did not care. All they needed was my name and birthdate in order to accomplish these atrocities. Instead of transferring me to the right police department, they had me hang up because I was not in their jurisdiction. Can you imagine this happening while your life was in danger? I ripped everyone a new one! I did get a police report number and the name of the officer who took the report - all while ripping him a new one, as well. The report includes the first name of my date and my driver's name along with his license plate. I kept asking for highway patrol, yet they refused to transfer me.

Then something told me how to get out of the situation: I needed to chant. I *blasted* the car for the next 20 minutes by chanting "Nam Myoho Renge Kyo" over and over again. It is my physical and spiritual right to chant/pray. My voice, my inner power, and my fortitude came like large waves while deeply penetrating the earth for all to hear. The roads swirled, dipped like quick sand, and I sank lower to the ocean floor, trying to free myself so that I could dance again. No one would listen, but I prevailed.

The mantra I chant surpasses all phenomena. I am in direct rhythm with my internal universe when I repeat the mantra throughout the day and recite two chapters of the Lotus Sutra to a mandala written in ancient Sanskrit. I am an enlightened being, and my soul manifests certain experiences that I must learn from before moving onto the next lesson in life, good or bad. When I began chanting, I activated from within my power and the physical universe. I was in direct universal alignment even though it appeared to not be so.

I rose from the ocean floor as my Buddhahood kicked in. It was the chanting of the mantra which helped me that night. It has always helped me gain wisdom, remain enlightened. As I rose, my crown chakra, my third eye, my intuition, my awareness, my realizations, all came upward and out until I was in that high vibrational vortex. I was able to evolve from my own power and caught my breath as I emerged from the black ocean. My ancestors were with me the entire time once I determined to fight the power of the drugs, the alcohol, the two evil men, and the wrong done to me by law enforcement. In this way, I determined my destiny - whereby, I wrote a new contract that states I will never go through this SHIT again! No more! Enough is Enough! And I will not ever give up on me.

The black ocean became my cape and I kept climbing the mountains until I could spiritually see. There was a dark thunderous cloud in my third eye where I could not physically see anything. My eyesight was hindered the entire time. In Buddhism, Shakymuni Buddha climbed to Eagle Peek. There is an ancient parable that describes how tired he was and he had 12 days to reach the top of the mountain in order to see the capital over the moon. On the 11th day, he wanted to stop. This was my 11th day. I had to reach the top of the mountain in order to see the capital over the moon. If I gave up, I would never know the good that could have been. So, I kept chanting.

On that 12th day, with the black ocean as my cape, it swept away anymore sexual violence that would occur now or in the future. By going through this, I lightened my negative karma into a heightened positive karma. My chanting evoked a spiritual awakening that eradicated a past life and current life of sexual violence. I revealed what needed to be revealed to myself so that I could learn and grow from this last and final experience. I determined that it will not ever happen again this feeling of being unsafe, the experience of being drugged, and that sexual assault will not ever be in my life again.

Clearly, even as an enlightened being, I can still manifest evil persons and experiences. At this point, I knew that the spiritual world, meaning all universal forces, would see me safely through. It was not going to be the physical world, such as law enforcement, that would uphold my right to be safe. It is "I" that had to do that for myself.

On that night, I overcame two evil forces. I could not get through to the police no matter how much I pounded my words into the phone to help me. In everyday life, I have felt this way spiritually. I have felt that spiritually I could not get through. The universal law is very strict. The more I doubt or disregard its existence, the more I doubt myself and my own existence. Then the more I call upon these types of experiences that shake me to my core in order for me to understand that I need to trust and believe spiritually. I have the ability to live my life without crisis, trauma, and assault; but I choose these occurrences when I ignore my gifts, my intuition, and my feelings. When this happens, I am in a low vibration. The more I humanize myself the more harsh human experiences I will have in my life.

Enlightenment is the highest universal vibration. The second highest vibration of the universe is love. When both come together as one, there is no sadness, fear, or anxiety. When we are in a high vibration, as humans, we are able to live in a moment of happiness, delight, and joy. It all comes from within us. We radiate as the sun. Anyone with negative causes will be dealt with either by the physical world, such as the police; or by the spiritual world, or both. The spiritual world encompasses everything: the angels, all the Buddha gods, all deities, our ancestors, and much more. *Nam Myoho Renge Kyo* activates the universe within me and without attachment to any outcome. In that moment and for lifetimes to come whatever needs to be changed will happen based on my confidence and belief. If I stay a mortal wrapped in an oasis of fear, detriment, and anger, then it is only "I" that I have to look to. Therefore, even when I step outside of the vibrational vortex and my vibration is low… It is then calling for that experience to happen that will help me to grow. In this moment of that incident, I became whole. I will no longer be able to half-love myself, to have such doubts of what I deserve, or allow myself to be victimized in any way. I have learned to master these experiences and to suffer endlessly. But I must further master my innate ability to heal without backsliding into yesteryears and furthermore, determine to be done with such experiences. I know from the depths of my soul that I changed my circumstances, my soul contract, and karmic bond, which is all the same.

"A plant, a tree, a pebble, a speck of dust—each has the Buddha nature, and each is endowed with cause and effect and with the function to manifest and the wisdom to realize its Buddha nature." *The Writings of Nichiren Daishonin, Volume 1, page 356*

I was dropped off by rideshare a half-hour after he was due to bring me home, meaning it took a full hour to get me home. Road construction with only one detour does not extend the trip that long. My ride share app froze at some point and I could not access help or safety features. He was dangerously driving, going off the road, weaving in between lanes when there were no cars, and purposely being in spots on the road that were dead zones for wi-fi.

My chanting ripped the rideshare driver a new one! At that moment, as the evil driver pulled up to my place, the light almost blinded me. I had reached the top of Eagle Peak, and I could rest my soul because a new and more fulfilling journey will begin. A journey of missions to complete, a journey of joy, gratitude, appreciation, and thankfulness. I left my black cape in the car and was embraced by my children who were on the 9-1-1 call and directing the different police departments the entire time. I was embraced with unconditional love.

Days later, I ripped the executive team of the ride share a new one! Their only concern was not for me, it was for the driver. When I told them they have no right trying to talk to me without an advocate present (know your rights), their only question was if the driver drugged me? Why? So, they can dismiss my allegations. My only justice has been the refund of my rideshare at a whopping $33! I was drugged and trying to tell the police while in motion that my rideshare driver was not safe and I was in extreme danger.

This is my story, this is my power, and I choose to be happy no matter what. I am not a victim, I am not only a survivor, I am simply me. I am a GODDESS! I am LOVE! I am the SUN! I am the UNIVERSE! My strength I gained physically as a child and thought I needed to suffer forever. As an adult, I gave unto myself my own strength as a spiritual being. Time collapsed, in that moment, I was no different whether one year's old and being raped, or as an adult being assaulted. Time collapsed into one because I could have remained "as is"; instead, I used a tool, the power of *Nam Myoho Renge Kyo*, to empower myself.

It was sure inner strength, tenacity, courage, knowing my rights, chanting, and knowing my power as a Goddess that made me get through it all. This happened on September 12th and 13th, 2023. I know now not to report anything to law enforcement, even though "91% of the victims of rape and sexual assault are female, and 9% are male," reported by The National Sexual Violence Resource Center. They know the statistics, too. I have always known that sexual assault or assault of any kind is not taken seriously and victim-blaming is what law enforcement has been trained to do, especially while racially profiling individuals. I have a police background. None of what I went through is of any surprise or anything new.

When I rise above and beyond physical circumstances as a supernatural being, same as Siddhartha Buddha, with my long oceanic black cape climbing the tallest mountains to see the beauty of the capital over the moon, the more experiences I will have that are ebb and flow. It is from muddy waters that I evolve into a beautiful lotus plant. The higher my vibration, my awareness, love, self-realization, the faster I can recognize these things and quelch it before it begins. But, if by chance, I am on a low vibration then it may become a karmic lesson that I must learn in order to move through, and beyond such experiences.

My voice is for all of us females to take care of ourselves and to prevail no matter what! To know your rights! Never Give Up! If the police would have shown up at the restaurant, they may have put me in jail for being on drugs - even without my consent. By the restaurant's own ignorance or untimely show of concern, I was protected. I am blessed.

Yes, I still believe in LOVE and I still believe there is a good man out there for me in the world; a man who contributes to my happiness, and I to his. Those of us who have not experienced external kindness, love, and compassion must realize it exists within us; that we must give it to ourselves, first.

I also believe online dating has become extremely criminal, scammish, and dangerous. Please be careful. Educate yourself - know your rights!

Niki Bell is on a mission to alleviate human suffering through education and empowerment, thus eliminating a life of sexual trafficking, violence, assaults and their long-term effects. As the Global Strategic Advisor to private investors, she represents over 100 industries, and works to establish economic stability, development, and a more lovingly conscious global village. Niki is deeply-involved in the preservation of land usage, minerals, and resources across the world, as well as within her local community creating jobs for ALL through worldwide investment projects. You can find her online at: **https://linktr.ee/ diosadevida**

THIS BUGS ME... LONNEE REY

Some things are obvious; others, not so much. It is the covert stuff that we need to take notice of these days. But how? How do we suss-out the insidious integration of suspiciously unsafe components in our foods? Fortunately, this chapter will show you how to turn up the sensitivity on your BS detector so you won't be unwittingly duped much longer.

{NOTE: A complete list of video links is available for download on http://officialrattledawake.com/ These are important pieces of news and report on more than title implies.}

Nicole Kidman, in a photoshoot for Vanity Fair, is eating four types of live bugs served on silver platters. How is this a thing? Bugs are for bait, not the plate. And yet, here it is, served-up for us as "the new normal."

Nicole Kidman Eats Bugs | Secret Talent Theatre | Vanity Fair (see links doc)

While it is true, "change is the only constant," we need to put our foot down on bugs. Crickey!

Finland is proud of their bread, boasting 70 *whole* ground crickets:
Bread made from crushed crickets launches in Finland (see links doc)

The house cricket, Acheta domesticus, commonly in bait and pet stores are reared in large commercial cricket factories or by local entrepreneurs. Gee, you'd hate to live next door to one of those factories, huh?

My advice is to start checking labels again. You might never eat crickets on purpose, but the truth is, here in the US, you may have already: cricket flour is popping up where you least expect it. And that's the point of this chapter: giving you a surefire way to 'sense' if that apple or chip is going to be good for you. I'm not being dramatic, just emphatic. There is a dire need to get up to speed pretty quickly, my friend. 'Far too much tomfoolery going on…

"Actually Foods Cheddar Cheese Puffs" lists organic cricket flour as an ingredient. Wait, hol' up a minute: does the word "organic" imply these are free-range, grassfed, pesticide-free crickets? Oh, what a relief. *Whole ground*, however, means their eyes and poop shoot are ground up into light and airy cheddar snacks. Mmmm mmm.

Does it mean these "organic" crickets are magically free from the four-inch long parasites I've seen tweezered out of live crickets? It does? Oh cool, pass me some of that mealworm dip, man.

The EU is permitting mealworm larvae in their foods - cuz that's a good idea for humans to eat, right? Oddly enough, the EU has refused to import much of the foods produced here in the US. What bugs them? Side-by-side ingredient comparisons for Doritos prove the US is obsessed with adding chemicals that other countries do not accept or use in the exact same product - but larvae is fine? https://www.naturalnews.com/2023-01-25-eu-authorities-approve-crickets-mealworms-in-food.html (see links doc)

This bugs me even though I don't eat it: Chick-Fil-A's Chicken Sandwich has 50 ingredients; 32 of them are lab-made. They used to post the ingredients list online, but recently, they pulled it. Hmmm. Aww, don't worry Chick-fil-A, smart consumers know you are not the only big box store serving up chemicals with your Frankenstein chicken.

We also know KFC was 3D-printing chicken nuggets before anyone else. All y'all are doing weird things to the stuff you call food. No wonder you don't allow your kids to eat at your restaurant. Fact.

What is 3D printed chicken made of?
Made out of lab-grown stem cells, 3D-printed meat is an edible rendering of a meat-like product created from an additive manufacturing process. Layer by layer, 3D-printed meat is constructed, or scaffolded, *from a bio-ink* that extrudes out of a 3D printer nozzle.

Ya might as well print a photo of a chicken nugget, spray it with some seasoning salt, crumble it up - I mean, reshape the paper into a nugget, and eat it.

Are you laughing, thinking, "Oh well, that doesn't affect me"? Maybe. Affected or not, we are all being subjected to the whims of unelected oddballs like Bill Gates and Klaus Schwab, a James Bond villain knock-off, who are running roughshod over our lives in many ways. The part about our food being messed with is what really bugs me. Gates donated $13M to The Guardian and bought himself a nice bunch of articles promoting his lab-grown meat and World Economic Forum narrative.

Check out this recent segment of "Redacted" on YouTube The WEF is HIDING bugs in these foods and you don't even know it | Redacted with Clayton Morris (see links doc)

Before you say this is just a conspiracy theory...just visit the WEF's website and read all the reports on eliminating meat in favor of bugs.

Gross! Eating bugs may give you parasites (see links doc)

Parasites were detected in 244 (81.33%) out of 300 (100%) examined insect farms. In 206 (68.67%) of the cases, the identified parasites were pathogenic for insects only; in 106 (35.33%) cases, parasites were potentially parasitic for animals; and in 91 (30.33%) cases, parasites were potentially pathogenic for humans. Edible insects are an underestimated reservoir of human and animal

Bugs are for bait, not your plate.

◆ ◆ ◆

And then there is the magnetic meat. What's that - you say you didn't see it on the news? Cue shock face. Tell-lie-vision. If you only get half the truth, what's the other half?

If you want to know more of what the real news is today, I have intentionally posted multiple platforms as reference links. I spent years discerning the shills from the sages. Do your own research. Stay abreast of changes in our food supply and policies that will impact you or your kids. They are already encouraging kids to eat bugs at some US schools. Yeah, no kidding.

Back to the magnetic meat. I'll let this video do ALL the talking. A *rattled awake* moment here was when the name brand, Simple Truth Organics, also tested positive for magnetism. I was like, 'Damn, there goes another one.'

MAGNETIC MEAT - TIM TRUTH (see links doc)

Jan 31, 2022 compilation of proof

This guy revisited Walmart in August 2023 to see if they were still selling magnetic meat. #SHORT (see links doc)

LADY TRIES TO HEAT SOME HAM IN A MICROWAVE

AND IT SPARKS LIKE CRAZY BECAUSE OF THE

METALS IN IT. Sept. 24, 2023 (see links doc)

Baby step: take a magnet with you to the grocery store. Test the product. If someone asks what you are doing, tell them. Say it forward. Rattle them awake, too.

Two baby steps: Say something out loud. My friend thinks nothing of showing other people within earshot that his magnet is sticking to all sorts of meat products. It gets attention and it forces the store manager to take action. Somebody has to call it for what it is. Magnetic meat is just wrong. And so is fake food.

You might be eating Bill Gates lab grown meat tonight | Redacted with Clayton Morris (see links doc)

For years I thought, "Surely, Shirley, there *has* to be a way for us to suss out these suspicious and shady practices."

The good news is THERE IS GOOD NEWS - a simple way for you to discern good from bad. That's the whole point of this chapter. Hang with me; I don't mean to gross you out before you finish reading. I promise you, there is a great solution to combat what these underhanded creeps, who have nothing good in mind but power and profits, are trying to slip into our food.

I'm not trying to freak anybody out here - I'm just being practical. Knowledge is power! When we know better, we can do better. Armed with the testing technique you will learn in this chapter, you will be prepared, not scared.

Unpacking the Groceries - a kitchen scene

"Honey? Where's the Heinz ketchup? Why did you get this other brand?"

He says, "I couldn't find it, Dear. I looked and looked for it."

Dear slaps her forehead in a 'V-8 moment' then says, "OHH, Honey, didn't you hear? After all these years, the Heinz label is now blue. No wonder you couldn't see it."

"Ohh, you know what, Dear? I actually saw a blue label ketchup, but I looked right past it - it wasn't familiar, you know?" She nods 'yes.'

Beliefs can make us blind. It's entirely possible that Honey may have never seen the Heinz Ketchup again, were he not told what to look for. Now that he knows what to look for, he will see it.

"Dear, I just can't believe they did that - it makes no sense." "I agree, Honey, but it is what it is."

Honey walks away, mildly disgusted at the changeover; shocked that someone in a board room somewhere thought that was a good idea. With a shoulder shrug, he mumbles, "Some things will never make sense; we just gotta deal with it, I guess." Honey couldn't see what was there the whole time.

The eyes are useless when the mind is blind.

I selected certain videos to cite visible proof; to educate the unaware, and train the eye. Cognitive dissonance, or, being so shocked that one refuses to acknowledge "what is," equates to a closed mind. A closed mind lets in no light. With all due respect to the "it's all good - this is supposed to happen and everything is fine," types, everything is not fine - unless you are happy to surrender your health, and freedom of choice, to control freaks. To believe the ship will magically right itself if we meditate, visualize the new earth hard enough, or pray that someone will appear (or take office) and take care of this insanity for us, is lovely, but it is also passive, wishful thinking.

When you wear rose-colored glasses, you miss the red flags.

Ignoring these things does not make them go away. While some proffer 'if you focus on the negative you get more negative,' the glaring opposite is true: by refusing to see what is already happening, it continues to happen. It IS happening, right now, under our collective noses, like it or not. It *should* make you mad, unless you're a robot. No, this is not "fine," and it bugs me.

The reality is, we are being bulldozed by apathetic creeps who are happy to let you sit and watch them destroy both your health and the planet itself. WE are carbon. The planet exists because of carbon. Who named these losers as leaders, anyway? Things are not as they seem, friends. If you dig, you will discover their premise of climate change has been debunked. Depending on when they compare temperatures, the earth is actually cooling. Follow the money behind these so-called "experts" and you will find their studies being funded by those who gain power and profit from the climate change narrative.

"He who controls the weather controls the world" - LBJ

Are you aware the US Air Force has openly stated their intentions to control all weather worldwide? This isn't a conspiracy theory. It is a conspiracy to manipulate, sure, but it is not a theory, it is fact. It is already happening. Gates thinks we need to dim the sun. Yeah, sure Bill:

WHY ARE WE ARE SEEING THE WEIRD SHAPED

CLOUDS IN THE SKY? - THIS IS THE CAUSE https://

www.bitchute.com/video/j047iB70UP3F/ (see links doc)

Watch "The Dimming" here
https://www.geoengineeringwatch.org/ (see links doc)

Regardless, pushing chemicals and bugs down our throats is vile. Clearly, 3D printed- or lab-grown "meat" is not a healthy alternative required to save the planet. The cost of chemicals required to do these things is preposterous - but it is nothing compared to the profits made at your expense: loss of health and freedom of choice. Yikes.

Ignorance is bliss...until it isn't.

Only through awareness and action can we make change happen with intention. It is up to us to question what we've been spoonfed - hopefully, it bugs you, too. Take action before taking another bite of baloney.

NOT APEELing

There is now a product coating organic and conventional produce that is made with toxic ingredients. It can't be washed off. Yes, organics have it now, too. Once again we have a Gates backed product being put into the mainstream. VOTE WITH YOUR FEET: shop at places who refuse to use this chemical derivative. Our bodies are not equipped to handle these known poisons.

Question "trust the science" narrative, puhleeze. This is the actual description and patent for Apeel:
"Described herein are methods of *sanitizing* and preserving produce and other agricultural products, for example for consumption as Ready-to-Eat. The methods can comprise treating the products with a sanitizing agent and forming a protective coating over the products. A method of treating produce, comprising a coating agent dissolved in a solvent, the solvent comprising a sanitizing agent: alcohol, ethanol, methanol, acetone, isopropanol, ethyl acetate. Heavy Metals: Palladium, Arsenic, Lead, Cadmium, Mercury."

 Method for preparing and preserving sanitized products: https://patents.google.com/patent/US20170332650A1/en

Look at the labels on your produce.
A LOT OF THE FOOD YOU EAT IS FAKE (see links doc)

Labels that begin with a nine are allegedly upholding organic growth standards. I say allegedly because now we have organic produce being coated with Apeel and other brand name derivatives - chemicals that do unnatural things like this:

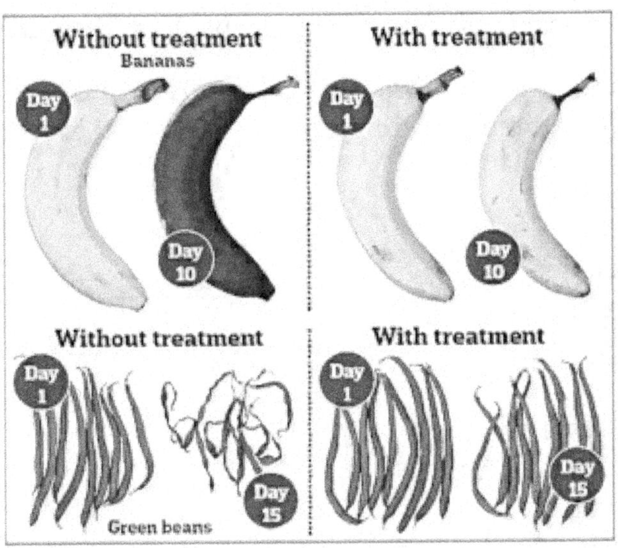

(image credit: Daily Mail)

Some consumers are growing concerned that Apeel-coated produce is off-gassing toxic substances. They report bugs dropping dead in the general area where the produce has been stored.

I guess you could plunk the bugs into your Apeel smoothie and give that a whirl, Shirl. ACK! Imagine what this is doing to your body.

PEELING BACK THE TRUTH ON APEEL (see links doc)

My hope is this chapter rattles you awake; that you share it with your network, family and friends. I want you to feel empowered with knowledge and inspired to act. *Tell* your grocer you won't be buying their Apeel-coated produce. If enough people refuse to buy it they will have to stop pushing it on us. There is a petition as well as its *ghastly* ingredients listed here: https://www.momsacrossamerica.com/_apeel (see links doc)

Store locator: https://www.apeel.com/find-us
Apeel is (or will be) available at the following grocers:

- Costco
- Trader Joes
- Gelsons
- Ralphs
- Sprouts
- Vons
- Walmart
- Whole Foods
- Kroger
- Harps Foods
- Wakefern
- Price Right
- Fairway Market
- Target
- Bristol Farms and more

Another thing to be on the lookout for is the change of labels that used to say GMO. They now say, "contains a BIOENGINEERED ingredient." We expect it, I guess, but what about this:

Wind turbine blades (54k tons waste per year) are being repurposed into gummy bears, and garbage plastics will soon become vanilla ice cream. Watch "The Crowhouse" on bitchute.com, episode "Looting the World" @1:03:05. Use the discernment technique shown later in this chapter to discern your way to - or away from, beautifully packaged lies.

◆ ◆ ◆

Sadly, this atrocity to our food supply is being dictated to us by people who have absolutely no authority over us, and yet they have installed themselves over us. These people are the real reason I wrote, "How to Deal with a Dumbass: what to do and say when they come your way." It was fueled by my taking an objective look at the global stage, noticing a piss-poor parade of clowns, then figuring out a way to respond to it without getting depressed, frankly.

"Think global, act local" took on a whole new meaning when I wrote that book because the only thing we can manage is our personal mindset and our personal reality. It is up to us who, and what, we let in the front door; what we buy with our money; what we put into our mouths; and how we take action as new things become known to us. Passivity does nothing but create more of the same: nothing. Silence = compliance.

I want you to think, what *can* I do? Plenty. Becoming aware of what is happening and taking action, being proactive versus reactive, makes it easier to implement solutions for yourself.

You might be wondering, *How* does this level of BS happen? *Who* is behind all of this? Here is a fascinating 15-minute overview showing you how these things happen on such a grand scale:

Dr.SHIVA™ LIVE: The Swarm – HOW the Few Control the Many.

What WE Do to Break Free. (see links doc)

This video, with over 5M views, went viral in spite of shadow-banning; a testament to the power of saying it forward.

It is time for us all to activate our innate power for positive change. No one is coming to save us from the clown parade. Besides, savior complexes won't put food on your table. Decisions are being made for us, covertly (until you learn where to look), by bonafide psychopaths. We have already witnessed how the FDA will recommend products that are not tested long enough for safety, the disastrous results, and built-in indemnity. There is no recourse, in other words.

When you know where to look, you will see "trust the science" people are back-peddling now with admissions of guilt that will blow your mind. You won't hear it on network tell-a-vision, of course. Check out bitchute.com. Channels like "The Crowhouse" (98k subscribers) and "Jim Crenshaw" (78k subs) with short videos that are hilarious, are recommended. On YouTube, "Off Grid with Doug and Stacy," homesteaders with a penchant for natural remedies as well as informed news updates, are worth your time. (see links doc)

There are what's called "reaction videos" on YouTube. This particular host curates TikTok videos and reminds us that we are in this together...so let us be aware of these things. Of course, it is always up to you to do your research. I'm not saying every video is the gospel truth, however, I know you will find them both entertaining and enlightening. NOTE: the opening video is not special effects - it is proof of scripted "news" being parroted on every channel: (see links

doc)
https://youtu.be/8LmfAMOEMp4?si=T4j6f4Fia9VcsAwA

In "Rattled Awake: Volume One" my chapter covered a jarring, rattled *awake* moment upon learning that nearly 2,000 food processing plants went >poof< all coincidentally by fire, in just the past year or so. A year ago the count was 20, but now look. sheesh From what I hear, they are not coming back anytime soon. Suspicious? Yep. Response: stock up now. Just do it wisely. Things have gotten scary-sketchy on the food front. Going in, heavily armed, (with knowledge), is whatcha gotta do these days.

1900 FOOD PROCESSING PLANTS HAVE BEEN DESTROYED IN THE PAST YEAR. (see links doc)

In that first chapter, I failed to mention the mass extermination of *tens of millions* of chickens and tens of thousands of cattle. This is a big concern, indeed. Still, it does not excuse this fake product being sold at your local Aldi & Walmart. Eggland's Best Organic Eggs are included:

Plastic Eggs at Walmart !!! (see links doc)

We can't really trust labels anymore. So what do we do? How do we make an informed decision?

Over 30 years ago, I experienced tremendous insights by being muscle tested. Based on kinesiology, it is your body's way of telling you if something is good or bad, true or not true. As you will see in this really cool video, the host is able to bust his son for lying. It's kind of funny, (bet his son isn't laughing), but it shows you how you can utilize this simple technique, among others, in a multitude of ways.

Learn to Muscle Test and the World Is In Your Hands!!!...Comments Required (see links doc)
(Click the video's description box to find other videos he made on muscle testing.)

I recommend practicing with a deck of cards so you can grow your intuitive muscle and muscle testing skills. Simply place a card face down and test yourself asking a yes or no question: "Is this a red card?" You could go even further and say 'is this a heart? club? spade? or diamond?' Practice the finger jiggle to see how good you get with playing cards. Grow confidence in your ability to assess quickly. You can't go wrong learning to trust in your body's innate and higher wisdom.

We are fortunate to have Melody Morris on LinkedIn. Her show, "Practical Spirituality Live" is co-hosted with the king of co-hosts, Eny Osung. DEF check out their audio events, every second Thursday of the month, 3pm EST. Melody, whose tagline reads, "I teach spiritual practices proven by modern neuroscience!" is a big fan of muscle testing. She is also on Facebook. I reckon listening to her will change your life, too.

So...it's time for the million-dollar question: Are you willing to stand in the produce department and do a quick finger jiggle to see if this is actually a safe product, or not? *Why not?* is really the question. You might inspire a movement, and, at the very least you'll be making wise choices for yourself and your family. Tip: I lower my hand into the grocery cart to 'finger jiggle.'

Choose not to trade your freedom for comfort. Watch "Jones Plantation." Best twenty bucks I've spent in a long time. The metaphors are mind-blowing. Your mature children will enjoy it, too. (see links doc)

◆ ◆ ◆

You are the solution

I know the things I've shared with you are really hard to stomach. (No pun intended.) It's vile, and is being implemented without our consent. Thanks to people like you who took the time to check out the videos and share the information, we can have a movement of awareness, action and change.

To do:

1. Get yourself a magnet, take it to the grocery store, and use it.
2. Get a deck of cards and test your muscle testing skills until you perfect them; then use them when making important decisions, moving forward.
3. *Tell* your grocer their use of Apeel means they don't get your money, it's that simple.
4. Read labels. Twice. Vote Frankenstein "foods" off the island: don't buy any of it.
5. Try this app: "Yuka" deciphers product labels and analyzes the health impact of food products and cosmetics. "Annie's Organics" products, 9 out of 10, are all poorly-rated. That fact alone should alert you to the need to reevaluate labels and brands.
6. Grow your own indoors: https://edengrowsystems.com/

This chapter is an F-bomb, of sorts, I know. Take a different perspective and you can shift into higher gear. We don't have to take this sh*t lying down. These new actions may seem awkward, like learning to ride a bicycle was, initially. Eventually, it got easier to do - with no hands, even.

Now that you know better, you can do better; you can take back authority over your life and make decisions in your favor. I hope you will "F" it and shift with the times.

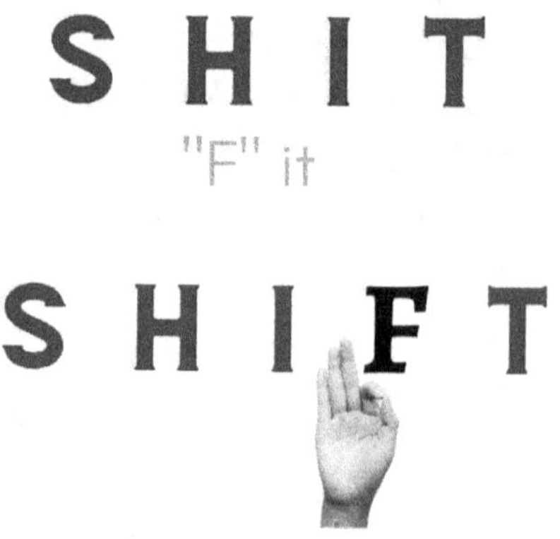

We simply need to activate our God-given powers of discernment, and enjoy the benefits that come *only through action.* The most capable hand is at the end of your wrist.

Think back to a wedding: the music starts and everyone is looking around, hoping someone will be the first to get up and start dancing. Once they do, and you have seen this - then others join in. A movement starts with one.

Somebody has to open the dance floor. Will it be you?

Each one, teach one. When we stand united, we are an empowered force of unlimited and exponential potential.

'One person can make a difference, and everyone

should try.' —John F. Kennedy

Lonnee Rey is on a mission to raise the voices of others whose stories will elevate, inspire and change our world for the better. She is a story development coach, concierge book producer, multi-show podcast host and author-message maestro. You can find "Rattled Awake: Volume One," "Life Lessons Learned From a Lousy Mother" and "Dumbass" on Amazon.

If you would like to share your Rattled Awake moment in an upcoming book, connect with her:

OfficialRattledAwake.com

AN OPEN INVITATION

The "Rattled Awake" movement is an ongoing series dedicated to promoting messages from everyday people on a mission to share their legacy, in print, forever.

The writing workshops continue to inspire both first-time writers as well as experienced writers - all of whom benefit from the collaboration as well as the training.

If you have ever wanted live coaching and help getting your thoughts down on paper, then out into the world, this is your chance.

"Don't die with the music still in you."
Dr. Wayne Dyer

Write one chapter - in one weekend - and enjoy the status "Co-author of the Best Seller, Rattled Awake" forever.

Visit OfficialRattledAwake.com for more information about the next workshop.

Schedule a chat with Lonnee Rey - together, you can hone-in on how to convey your Rattled Awake moment.